NEXT CHAPTER BOOK CLUB

A Model Community Literacy Program for People with Intellectual Disabilities

Tom Fish, PhD, LISW & Paula Rabidoux, PhD/CCC

with Jillian Ober, MA, CRC & Vicki L. W. Graff, BA, BEd

Woodbine House ■ 2009

All rights reserved under International and Pan-American copyright conventions. Published in the United States of America by Woodbine House, Inc., 6510 Bells Mill Rd., Bethesda, MD 20817. 800-843-7323. www.woodbinehouse.com

Library of Congress Cataloging-in-Publication Data

Fish, Thomas R.
  Next Chapter Book Club : a model community literacy program for people with intellectual disabilities / Thomas R. Fish, Paula Rabidoux ; with Jillian Ober and Vicki L.W. Graff.
     p. cm.
  Includes bibliographical references and index.
  ISBN 978-1-890627-79-9
  1. People with mental disabilities--Social networks. 2. Book clubs (Discussion groups) 3. Group reading. 4. Functional literacy. I. Rabidoux, Paula. II. Title.
  HV3004.F545 2009
  367--dc22

                                                                                                  2009018433

Manufactured in the United States of America

10   9   8   7   6   5   4   3   2   1

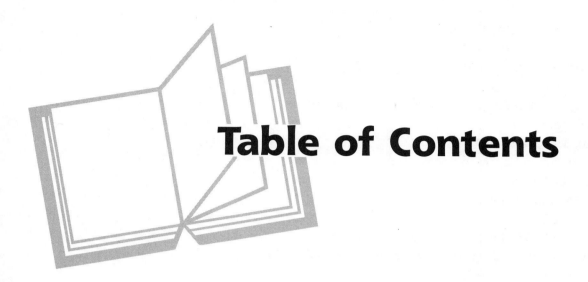

Table of Contents

Foreword / vii

Preface / ix

Acknowledgments / xiii

Introduction / xv

1. What Is the Next Chapter Book Club? / 1

How Does the Next Chapter Book Club Work?

What Are the Objectives of the Next Chapter Book Club?

Who Participates in the Next Chapter Book Club?

Next Chapter Book Club Organizational Chart

How Is the Next Chapter Book Club Organized?

Who Leads the Next Chapter Book Club?

Who Benefits From the Next Chapter Book Club?

2. Why Should You Start a Next Chapter Book Club in Your Community? / 7

The Next Chapter Book Club Model

Reciprocal Relationships in the NCBC Model

3. Who Are NCBC Affiliates? / 15

Profiles of NCBC Affiliates

Current NCBC Affiliates

4. What Happens at an NCBC Affiliate Training Workshop? / 21

Getting Started

The Affiliate Training Workshop

Feedback From Workshop Participants

5. How Do Local Program Coordinators Run an NCBC Program? / 27

Who Can Be a Program Coordinator?

Recruiting

Training

Retention

Scheduling

Monitoring, Support, and Evaluation
Book and Supply Inventory
Making Book Accommodations
Finding Host Sites
Community Collaborations and Program Development
Program Funding

6. Who Are NCBC Members? / 37
How Do We Recruit New Members?
Profiles of NCBC Members' Literacy Levels
Who Are Peer Activity Leaders (PALs)?
Profiles of NCBC PALs
How Well Has the PAL Program Worked?

7. What Do NCBC Members Want To Know About Their Club? / 49
A Book Club: "What A Novel Idea"
Our Members Speak!

8. Who Are NCBC Facilitators? / 55
Why Do We Recruit Volunteers?
What Are the Benefits of Volunteering?
Why Do NCBC Facilitators Volunteer?
Why Do We Recruit Two or More Facilitators for Each Club?
How Does This Experience Compare with What Facilitators Expect?
How Does This Experience Relate to Other Aspects of Facilitators' Lives?
What Would Current Facilitators Say to Prospective Ones?
Profiles of NCBC Facilitators

9. What Do NCBC Facilitators Do? / 67
Step 1: Examine Your Motivation for Becoming an NCBC Facilitator
Step 2: Prepare Yourself and Your Club
Step 3: Facilitate Your Group
Step 4: Become Involved in Recruiting New NCBC Members and Facilitators

10. What Are NCBC Host Sites? / 79
What Does a Host Site Do?
What Are the Benefits to Host Sites?
How Do Host Sites Respond to the NCBC?
Why Not Meet in Libraries and Community Centers?
What Are the Disadvantages of Bookstores and Cafés?
What About Meeting in Restaurants?
Are There Exceptions to the NCBC Host Site Rule?
Profiles of NCBC Host Sites
How Do I Select a Host Site?
How Should I Approach a Host Site Manager?
Profile of an NCBC Host Site Manager

11. What Is the Role of Families and Support Staff? / 91

12. What Strategies and Activities Do Book Clubs Use? / 95
Strategies and Activities That Encourage Reading

Strategies and Activities That Encourage Social Interaction
Strategies and Activities That Increase Community Inclusion

13. How Do You Market and Promote the NCBC Program? / 121
Reaching Out to Families, Support Staff, and Service Coordinators
Reaching Out to Service Agencies and Advocacy Organizations
Reaching Out to People with Intellectual Disabilities
How To Approach Funding Sources and Community Organizations

14. How Can You Evaluate the NCBC Program? / 127
Literacy Evaluations
Family Members and Support Staff Evaluations
Questions for Member Interviews
Questions for Facilitator Interviews
Community Inclusion Surveys

15. Conclusion: What's the Next Chapter? / 133

16. Frequently Asked Questions and Special Considerations / 135
Club Operations
Composition
Group Dynamics
Strategies

NCBC Contact Information / 143

Glossary / 145

References / 149

Resources / 155

Appendices / 162
A: Next Chapter Book Club Library / 163
B: Member Intake Form / 165
C: Facilitator Intake Form / 166
D: Facilitator Position Description / 167
E: Monthly Facilitator Report / 168
F: Member End-of-Book Survey / 171
G: Certificate of Accomplishment / 172
H: Five-Level Scale of Literacy Skills / 173
I: ECO-NCBC Literacy Observations / 174
J: Family/Staff Expectations Survey / 175
K: Family/Staff Satisfaction Survey / 177
L: Questions for Member Interviews / 180
M: Chuckie's Questionnaire / 182
N: Questions for Facilitator Interviews / 184
O: Community Inclusion Survey for Members BEFORE Book Club / 186
P: Community Inclusion-Location Survey for Members AFTER Book Club / 189
Q: Community Living Attitudes Scale (Adapted) / 193
R: *Western Springs Suburban Life* article: "Unique book club started for young adults" / 195

Index / 197

Foreword

A quote by Carl Sandburg is inscribed on an entrance portal of the university where I teach: "Nothing happens unless first a dream." The quote is meant to inspire students as they enter the campus each day. But I find it equally inspiring, and it certainly describes how Next Chapter Book Club came to St. Louis.

My daughter, Andrea, is a delightful young woman with Down syndrome. Two years ago, as we were preparing for her transition from high school to life as an adult, we mapped out her goals. There were three: finding a job, building a strong network of friends, and maintaining the literacy skills she acquired in school. We found a variety of support systems in place to assist people with intellectual disabilities (ID) to find employment and engage in social activities. But there were no resources related to literacy after high school.

Andrea has always loved books. She has a large collection at home and enjoys visiting bookstores and the local library. I thought that she would love to participate in a book club. So I spent much of a snowy January day writing email inquiries to local and national organizations, asking if anyone knew about book clubs for people with intellectual disabilities. Every response was the same: "No, but what a great idea!" In frustration, I turned to a colleague, Dr. Philip Ferguson, who is the E. Desmond Lee Professor of Education for Children with Disabilities. I asked if he would distribute an email inquiry to his extensive network of contacts. A few weeks later I received a brief message that simply said, "I think there's something going on at the Ohio State University Nisonger Center."

And indeed, there was something truly wonderful going on at the Nisonger Center. As soon as I learned about Next Chapter Book Clubs, I asked if they would please consider expanding beyond Ohio and into the St. Louis area.

Next Chapter Book Club presented an extraordinary opportunity for the University of Missouri-St. Louis to partner with local organizations that serve people with intellectual disabilities. The Next Chapter Book Club Partnership of Greater St. Louis/St. Charles includes UM-St. Louis, the Down Syndrome Association of Greater St. Louis, St. Louis ARC, and Life Skills. To date, our partnership has launched nine book clubs in the greater St. Louis metropolitan area.

Andrea has been a member of one of the St. Louis-area book clubs for two years now. She looks forward to Thursday nights, when she shares an hour with her book club friends, a good book, and a cup of hot chocolate. They read, they talk, they laugh together. Much like the inscription on the portal of the campus where I teach, the book clubs are an inspiration to the Thursday night bookstore crowd.

Deborah Baldini, PhD
University of Missouri-St. Louis

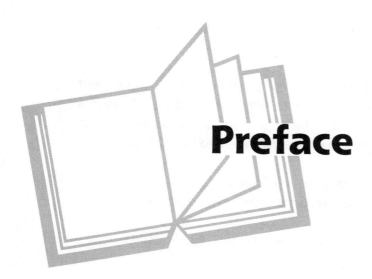

Preface

The Next Chapter Book Club (NCBC) is committed to promoting literacy and social connection experiences for adolescents and adults with intellectual disabilities (ID) that encourage friendship and lifelong learning within a community-based setting.

We often hear the terms *community inclusion*, *socialization*, *self-determination*, and *self-advocacy* when talking about adolescents and adults with intellectual disabilities (formerly referred to as mental retardation). Next Chapter Book Clubs offer real-life examples of these terms and ideologies in action. The clubs allow people a chance to be part of the community in a real and meaningful way. Rather than an occasional community outing, the book clubs are purposeful gatherings of the same people every week.

Self-Determination

Members determine practically all aspects of their participation in the NCBC. They decide whether to join, which club they join, and if they want to continue. Sometimes members take a break from their club to attend other events or programs and then return. Along with their fellow club members, they choose which books to read and how much they want to read. They decide how much and how often to talk during the club, consistent with courtesy to others.

Members also select and order their own refreshments. If members forget to bring money, facilitators encourage them to do so the following week. Facilitators generally do not loan members money or order drinks for them, unless a member requests assistance. Parents, support staff, and facilitators often note how members who had never ordered their own food before learn how to do it as part of their participation in the NCBC.

Essentially, the NCBC is all about self-determination. We hope the numerous choices members make carry over to other areas of their living and working in the community.

Community Inclusion

Members experience community inclusion by doing a purposeful activity, meeting and gathering with members and friends. Interacting with employees and customers in a bookstore or café adds another dimension. Finally, doing what others do—reading, hanging out, having money, and ordering a drink—helps make the experience inclusive and meaningful.

> *They appear to be very comfortable in the community setting. Some of the group members order their own refreshments and many feel comfortable roaming the bookstore alone, browsing, and using the restroom.*
>
> —*Amy E, co-facilitator, Columbus, Ohio*

Self-Advocacy

Several aspects of the NCBC promote self-advocacy:

- expressing ideas and opinions in the club
- making sure whoever is supposed to bring a member to the book club does so
- learning from and teaching others
- talking about one's wants and needs

To date, the NCBC has benefited more than 600 participants with ID in over 130 clubs in fifty-five cities in the United States, three cities in Canada, and four cities in Germany. We trust that this experience will enrich the lives of all those involved in your area.

Personal Note From Tom Fish:

Sometimes things just make sense, and they don't need to be complicated. I came up with the idea for the Next Chapter Book Club with those sentiments in mind. The idea behind the NCBC is actually pretty simple. Our book clubs are based on having fun, being in the community, and learning something along the way. Sure, it takes organization, commitment, and support, but most successful programs require those ingredients. The beauty of the NCBC is that the members and facilitators make it happen. And things almost always go very smoothly.

I have over thirty years of experience as a social worker and educator in the disability field, mostly at The Ohio State University Nisonger Center. Much of my time is devoted to training graduate students from multiple disciplines about the family and community aspects of disabilities. I am always thinking about ways to improve the quality of life for people with disabilities and their families. My inspiration for the book clubs stemmed from seeing more people with disabilities out in the community, but rarely noticing them interacting with one another. It's one thing to do a group outing, yet entirely another to engage socially and function in a purposeful activity together right smack dab in the middle of the community, where other people are. So I guess you could say the book clubs are about equality and meaning. They strive to give teeth to the term "community inclusion" and recognize that people with disabilities at all ages and all levels of functioning are capable of learning new things.

On a personal note, I had many challenges learning, both as a child and as an adolescent. School for me was an unpleasant experience, to say the least. The idea of picking up a book for enjoyment—reading for fun—was completely foreign to me. So how did I ever come up with the idea that people with intellectual disabilities might be interested in and/or capable of reading?

I think the answer lies in the fact that book clubs take place in the larger community. Reading like this is part of an enjoyable experience rather than doing it alone in an isolated setting. I actually wrote most of my dissertation in McDonald's, so holding book clubs in bookstores and cafés was a no-brainer for me. And only once that we know of has a bookstore or café expressed any resistance to hosting a book club. So, the book clubs work because they are social, fun, and they promote learning for everyone involved. Not a bad combination, right?

As you read this book, we hope at some point a light will go off in your head and you'll think to yourself, "That's kind of neat." And after the light goes off, we urge you to start or advocate for a club in your area.

Personal Note From Paula Rabidoux:

Tom and I bring different experiences to NCBC. I have studied and written about storybook interactions between children with disabilities and their parents and have been teaching on the connections between language and literacy for several years. In many ways the transition to thinking about lifelong learning and adolescents/adults with intellectual disabilities fits perfectly with how I have been thinking about early language and literacy development. For both parents and children, and for NCBC members, the social context of literacy defines the event. We can have an enjoyable, interactive, communicative, and learning experience, or we can avoid books and everything to do with them. As we were developing NCBC, we incorporated many of the interaction principles we learned from our work with parents of young children during storybook interactions and adapted them for our NCBC groups: respond to members' comments, wait for a member to do or say something, follow a member's conversational lead, and have each member contribute about the same amount so no one dominates or controls the interaction. Developing an interactive literacy experience seemed similar for both groups. Integrating members with diverse literacy and social communicative skills has been surprisingly easy. More accomplished readers assist less accomplished, more social members engage less social members, and members who have fewer community interaction skills learn from those who have more and eventually interact in their communities. The members and facilitators of NCBC have created literacy communities where friendships are made, experiences are shared, and lives are enriched.

My personal literacy journey is wedded closely to a love for and desire to read. Some of my fondest early memories focus around books: being read to as a young child, reading ahead in class, and going to the public library and reading everything I could find on whatever topic interested me. Later, as an adult with my own family, we developed family traditions visiting bookstores and libraries, sharing books we enjoyed, and talking about characters, ideas, and stories. It now seems so apparent that people with intellectual disabilities would want to develop and share similar personal and community bonds. Perhaps this is why Tom's idea about a book club for everyone has thrilled so many. Everyone is included, everyone participates in whatever ways they can, and we all learn something new. I challenge you to give a NCBC a try, but beware, once you start, you may not want to stop.

Acknowledgments

We would like to personally thank all of the people who brought so much laughter and work to this project over the years. This book was made possible because a small group of parents, professionals, and consumers believed that adults with intellectual disabilities can and do want to read together in community bookstores and cafés. They met with us almost weekly for five months to brainstorm and develop the book club program. Our deepest gratitude goes to Peggy Martin, Steve Cooley, Cara Schauer, Randy Cuenot, Trisha Harp, Lynn Bartels, Jane Tragenovski, and Jeff Davis. We are forever in debt to Melissa Gourley, who ran the program for the first year, and to Tom's son, Roger Fish, age sixteen, who suggested one night at dinner that we name it the Next Chapter Book Club.

Thank you to Joan Kaderavek for her passionate and eloquent comparison of the accomplishments of NCBC members to those of Special Olympic athletes. Our sincerest thanks go to Emily Savors and all of the other wonderful people at The Columbus Foundation, who believed in and supported this project from its inception. We extend very special thanks to Dr. Steven Reiss, Director of The Ohio State University (OSU) Nisonger Center, who encouraged us in every way possible and contributed extremely valuable suggestions. We also recognize the incredible artistic contributions to the Next Chapter Book Club of Richard Aschenbrand, who designed our logo, and Lou Venneri, who has helped us market the program.

Then there is our valued Program Manager, Vicki Graff, who works tirelessly to promote, organize, and monitor the program. We also thank Vicki for her technical expertise and editorial skills. The NCBC simply would not be what it is today without the devotion and brilliance of our Program Manager (formerly Program Coordinator), Jillian Ober. We thank Jillian from the bottom of our collective hearts, because she is the glue that holds everything together and the spirit that keeps us moving forward.

For their support and guidance along the way we appreciate Susan Havercamp, Beth Sweigheimer, Jim Lynch, and several people at the Franklin County Board of MR/DD, including Frank

New and Marcy Samuel. We are also in debt to Ms. Anke Gross, who interned with our program for a year and has since formed several clubs in her home country, Germany.

Lastly, we are enormously indebted to all the book club facilitators across the country, who volunteer their time weekly and generously contribute their energy and ideas. As for our members, their enjoyment of the program and real sense of purpose always reinforce our desire to grow the program and make it better. Together we have been having fun and reading some really good books.

Introduction

We are pleased to introduce you to the Next Chapter Book Club (NCBC). This book will provide you with helpful information, whatever your level of involvement with the NCBC. Everyone will learn how the program got started and how it works (Chapter 1). Affiliate organizations will learn the rationale for the formation of this type of program for people with intellectual disabilities (ID), also called developmental disabilities (DD) (Chapter 2). You can also read profiles of several affiliates (Chapter 3) and learn how the affiliate training workshops work (Chapter 4). As a program coordinator, you'll find the information you need to conduct this program in your area (Chapter 5).

You can find out who the members are and read several of their profiles (Chapter 6). If you are a prospective or current member, you can find out what to expect and read tips to help you get the most out of your club (Chapter 7). For potential volunteers, we offer reasons to facilitate a Next Chapter Book Club and profiles of current and former facilitators (Chapter 8). If you're one of our active facilitators, please see our step-by-step guide to managing your group and having fun (Chapter 9), and our extensive descriptions of strategies and activities that clubs can use (Chapter 12). (These are also available for printing out from the included CD-ROM.) Family members and support staff will gain a sense of the important role they play in helping members participate (Chapter 11).

Host sites will learn the benefits of welcoming an NCBC group into their businesses (Chapter 10). For all those interested in literacy, social connections, and community inclusion for people with ID, the book will serve as a platform for launching further creative efforts locally (Chapters 13, 14, and 15). Lastly, we answer frequently asked questions and discuss special considerations (Chapter 16).

Following the chapters are NCBC contact information, a glossary of terms, references, resources, appendices, and an index. The appendices are also available for printing out from the CD-ROM included.

Note that for the sake of impartiality, we have alternated gender pronouns chapter by chapter. Further, for privacy reasons, we have changed some names throughout.

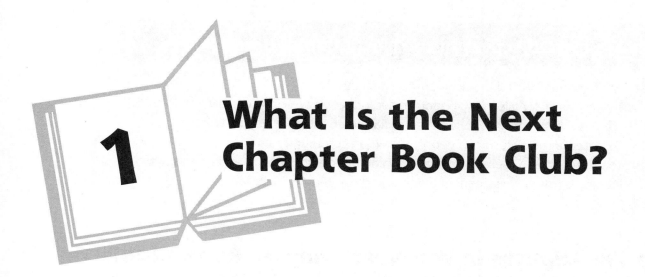

1 What Is the Next Chapter Book Club?

Unlike other book clubs, the Next Chapter Book Club (NCBC) provides opportunities for people with intellectual disabilities (ID) to read together and learn to read, talk about books, and make friends in a fun, community setting. The NCBC was established in June 2002 by a committee dedicated to lifelong learning and community inclusion for people with mental retardation and developmental disabilities (MR/DD). This committee consisted of Tom Fish of The Ohio State University Nisonger Center along with representatives from the Ohio Department of MR/DD, the Franklin County Board of MR/DD, Borders Books and Music, two individuals with ID, and a graduate student.

The committee had a discussion about the prevailing assumption that adults with intellectual disabilities are not readers, nor are they interested in lifelong learning. The group also discussed the isolation and segregation experienced by so many adults with disabilities who are living in, but not a part of, their communities. Committee members suggested that it would be fun for people with ID to participate in book clubs in a community setting such as a bookstore or café. Thus, the NCBC was designed to be an inclusive literacy experience for people with ID, regardless of reading ability.

How Does the Next Chapter Book Club Work?

The premise is simple: A group of five to eight people with intellectual disabilities, regardless of their reading skills, gather with two volunteer facilitators in a local bookstore, coffee shop, or café to read aloud and discuss a book for one hour a week. Much like members of any other book club, NCBC members choose how they want to structure their club and which books they want to read. Books in the NCBC library include adapted classic novels, such as *The Secret Garden* and *Treasure Island*, as well as current, popular fiction and nonfiction. (See a more complete list in Appendix A.) Members are learning, making friends, and having a lot of fun doing it!

Next Chapter Book Club
Library

Adapted Classics
A Christmas Carol
A Little Princess
A Wind in the Door
A Wrinkle in Time
Alice's Adventures in Wonderland
Anne of Green Gables
Anne Of Green Gables—
   Christmas Stories
Around the World in 80 Days
Black Beauty
Charlotte's Web

The Adventu
The Adventu
The Adventu
The Adventu
The Call of th
The Legend
The Lion, the
   Wardrobe
The Secret G
The Story of
The Story of

Appendix A *(p. 163)*

What Are the Objectives of the Next Chapter Book Club?

The Next Chapter Book Club has four primary objectives:
1. To increase lifelong learning opportunities for people with intellectual disabilities (ID)
2. To increase meaningful literacy and social experiences for people with ID
3. To increase the inclusion of people with ID in community settings
4. To develop and disseminate nationally and internationally a model program for literacy learning, social connectedness, and community inclusion

Who Participates in the Next Chapter Book Club?

Anyone can participate, whatever their reading or ability level. People without disabilities can also participate. NCBC members range from those who read well to those who require significant support.

NCBC started with two pilot groups, both consisting of six members with ID and two volunteer facilitators. One group chose to read *Harry Potter and the Sorcerer's Stone*; the other chose *Charlotte's Web*. Both clubs met weekly for one hour in the café at Borders Books and Music in Columbus, Ohio. The overwhelming success of the pilot groups demonstrated the benefits of expanding this program. All pilot members enjoyed the book club and wanted to continue to participate after they finished their books. The facilitators loved the experience and were amazed by all the dynamics that take place in the meetings.

> *Laura was one of the founding members and took part in initial meetings. She now belongs to three different clubs. She says, 'It's fun.' Because of her physical disabilities, Laura requires round-the-clock care. She has an average of six helpers; every eight hours there's a shift change. In addition to her book clubs, Laura has selected a book to read with each of her helpers! She knows which book she's reading with each person.*
> —Jan D, parent and legal guardian, Columbus, Ohio

By the end of 2004 (within two years of starting the program), we had 115 NCBC members in central Ohio. Forty-five percent of members (n = 52) were male and 55 percent were female (n = 63). Ages ranged from 17 to 82 years with an average age of 38.3 years. More than 95 percent of NCBC members were eligible for services through their local county board system. (Ohio has a county-based system for providing residential, educational, employment, and social services for people with developmental disabilities. Each county is a member of the Ohio Association of County Boards of Mental Retardation and Developmental Disabilities.)

The majority of members were not what is considered "conventionally literate." This means they were unable to independently read and understand most text (Kaderavek & Rabidoux, 2004). Because no appropriate tool was available to help us understand the literacy skills of the NCBC members, we devised a Five-Level Scale of Literacy Skills (Appendix H). Table 1 shows the reading

© 2004 Greg Sailor

levels of forty-five members in the summer 2004, based on the ratings of one facilitator from each group using the scale within three weeks from the start of the group.

These data suggest that 54 percent of members demonstrated "emergent" literacy skills that require a high level of social support (Levels I, II, and III) and 46 percent demonstrated some level of functional, independent literacy (Levels IV and V). Emergent literacy as used here describes the range of literacy activities developed cooperatively with interactive partners or in social/cultural contexts (Burns, Griffin, & Snow, 1999).

> *No matter how the session goes, everybody, even if they didn't know what they were doing, or they couldn't read as much as they would have liked, they're always like, 'Oh, boy, I'm coming back next week!'*
>
> —*Suzzanne F, co-facilitator, Columbus, Ohio*

Table 1.   Description of reading levels of forty-five NCBC members in 2004.

Reading Level	Percentage of Members Rated
Level I—no letter recognition or understanding of written language	20% (n = 9)
Level II—recognizes and understands letters	16% (n = 7)
Level III—reads and understands single words	18% (n = 8)
Level IV—reads and understands sentences	13% (n = 6)
Level V—reads and understands paragraphs	33% (n = 15)

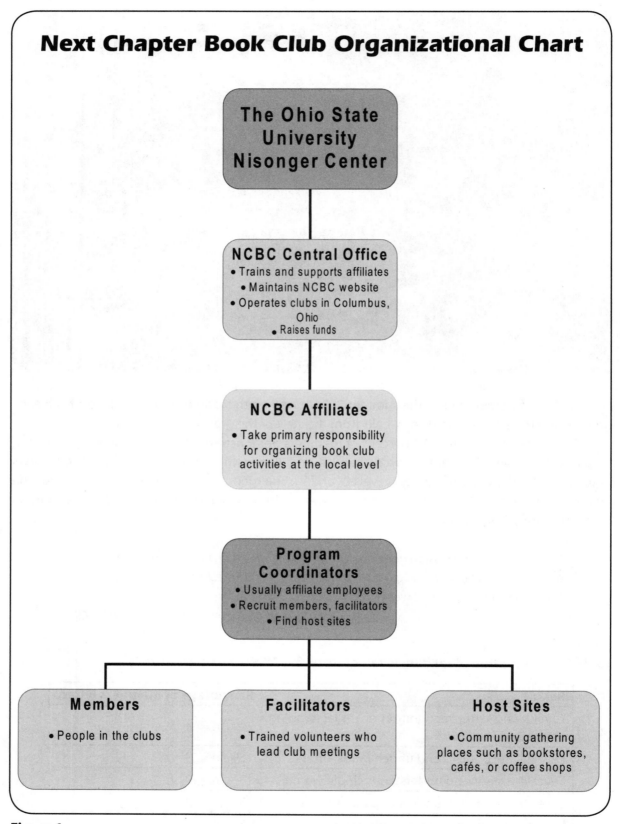

Next Chapter Book Club Organizational Chart

The Ohio State University Nisonger Center

NCBC Central Office
- Trains and supports affiliates
- Maintains NCBC website
- Operates clubs in Columbus, Ohio
- Raises funds

NCBC Affiliates
- Take primary responsibility for organizing book club activities at the local level

Program Coordinators
- Usually affiliate employees
- Recruit members, facilitators
- Find host sites

Members
- People in the clubs

Facilitators
- Trained volunteers who lead club meetings

Host Sites
- Community gathering places such as bookstores, cafés, or coffee shops

Figure 1

How Is the Next Chapter Book Club Organized?

As the organizational chart in Figure 1 shows, the NCBC is based at The Ohio State University Nisonger Center, part of a consortium of University Centers for Excellence in Developmental Disabilities. The Central Office staff consists of Program Director, Tom Fish, Program Managers Jillian Ober and Vicki Graff, and Literacy Specialist, Paula Rabidoux. The NCBC Central Office coordinates and promotes the program nationally and internationally. This involves the following tasks:

- training, supporting, and providing technical assistance to local organizations, called NCBC affiliates;
- maintaining the website, www.nextchapterbookclub.org;
- operating from eighteen to twenty clubs in the Columbus, Ohio, area;
- raising funds through grants and donations to support the Central Office; and
- conducting research and evaluations regarding the effectiveness of the clubs.

NCBC affiliates take primary responsibility for organizing book club activities at the local level. This includes employing a program coordinator, who is responsible for recruiting and placing members; recruiting and training volunteers; and finding host sites (locations for club meetings). Affiliates also raise funds and promote the NCBC program in their area.

Who Leads the Next Chapter Book Club?

Two or more volunteers trained by NCBC staff facilitate each group. Facilitator training consists of a sixty- to ninety-minute session with NCBC staff, wherein volunteers view a training curriculum via a slide presentation and review a manual (summarized in Chapter 9 of this book). The NCBC Central Office also provides ongoing training, with periodic educational and social events as well as resources available on a secure area of our website, www.nextchapterbookclub.org. Volunteer facilitators include high school and college students, parents, siblings, employees, business owners, professionals, retirees, and people with disabilities.

Each facilitator establishes a positive working relationship with his co-facilitator. Once a month they provide feedback on the club's meetings to the program coordinator. The primary responsibility of each facilitator is to maintain a comfortable and welcoming atmosphere where members are free to express themselves. A variety of strategies are used to support members based on their communicative and literacy abilities, including the following:

- encouraging members to take turns and respond to each other;
- communicating about an activity and showing members how to communicate and respond;

- engaging members emotionally, listening to members, and understanding what is meaningful to them;
- accepting actions, such as following along with bookmarks and turning pages, as meaningful;
- treating events in books as bridges to stories about members' lives;
- sounding out words and using "echo reading" with members who may need extra help (see Chapter 12); and
- encouraging an array of appropriate literacy behaviors.

After observing and taking detailed notes on one particular club, NCBC staff recommended that each week, one facilitator focus his attention on literacy activities while the other focus on social interactions among group members. (Much more information on what goes into being a facilitator is discussed in Chapters 8 and 9.)

> *I think at almost every Monday night meeting I see something new or learn something new about the members that makes me think, 'Wow, there's really some ability at that table.' That's the thing I keep walking away with; these folks have a lot to contribute.*
>
> —*Mike F, co-facilitator, Columbus, Ohio*

Who Benefits From the Next Chapter Book Club?

NCBC has been received positively by all parties involved. We have obtained letters of support from host sites, volunteer facilitators, members, families, and support staff. All view the NCBC as a positive addition to their lives, careers, and businesses. The enjoyment expressed by members and volunteer facilitators has spread throughout the ID community, resulting in a high demand for the development of additional book clubs. One unexpected outcome has been the extent to which the NCBC has increased public awareness of persons with ID in the community. Facilitators report being approached by people requesting further information about what the book clubs are for, how they operate, and how to become involved.

We're also spreading the NCBC model around North America and in Europe! During 2006 and 2007 we conducted training workshops and opened new chapters in Arizona, Idaho, Illinois, Indiana, Louisiana, Massachusetts, Missouri, New Jersey, New York, many counties in Ohio, Pennsylvania, Rhode Island, Virginia, and Wisconsin. We also started clubs in Bonn and Cologne, Germany. In 2008 we added clubs in California and expanded to communities in Ontario and British Columbia, Canada, as well.

> *Michaela is a member who usually only reads the back covers of books that seem interesting and doesn't read the whole book. Christiane, the facilitator, told Michaela that the back cover is only there to get one interested in the book and that she should start reading one of the books. After being in the NCBC for two months, Michaela told Christiane that she decided to take one of the books home to read it. Once she started, she couldn't stop, because it was so interesting.*
>
> —*Anke G, program coordinator, Cologne, Germany*

2 Why Should You Start a Next Chapter Book Club in Your Community?

Learning never ends—but some people have more opportunities than others. In the United States, people with ID leave the formal education system with few (if any) expectations that they will continue to learn academically or socially. Those adults who may express an interest in further literacy learning often find themselves referred to adult basic education programs, where staff may be ill-prepared to work with adults with ID. And if someone successfully locates a reading tutoring program, it is generally designed as a solitary learning activity that rarely meets the needs many people with ID have for social learning and community participation. Thus, even when learning opportunities are available, they most often occur without a social context.

History indicates that adults with ID have repeatedly been discouraged from or denied opportunities to engage in nonsegregated, inclusive community life. Although we have made progress in community living, competitive employment, and social integration, people with ID rarely participate in the fabric of community activities, despite living and working in communities (National Institute for Literacy, 1997). As many investigators have noted, living *in* the community is not the same as being a *part of* the community. Community inclusion needs to extend beyond one's residence, place of employment, and education; it must include interacting and forming relationships with other community members as well as belonging to clubs and organizations (Renzaglia et al., 2003). These are among the reasons we started the Next Chapter Book Club in 2002.

The Next Chapter Book Club Model

We believe that active participation in a book club can support community inclusion, self-determination, and literacy learning. The NCBC provides adults with ID an opportunity to make social connections in a community environment, to improve self-esteem and literacy skills, and to continue to learn.

The Next Chapter Book Club Model

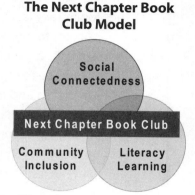

Figure 2

Literacy

We currently have limited theoretical and practical knowledge about how adults with ID might maintain and develop literacy skills beyond school. Research suggests that participation in reading as a leisure activity *declines* significantly for many young adults with ID after they leave the structured support of the educational system (Wagner et al., 2004). In 1995, The Roeher Institute published a series of monographs based on interviews of people with ID regarding their experiences with literacy instruction. The common recurring themes expressed by these participants included exclusion and segregation from the mainstream, the presumption of illness, discrimination, poverty, loneliness, and vulnerability to abuse and violence. These are some of the barriers people with ID encounter when they are interested in learning, literacy, and becoming part of a community. The Next Chapter Book Club promotes increased participation in literacy socialization as one mechanism to address and alter these inequities.

One objective of the NCBC program is to develop an inclusive working model of adult literacy learning for people with ID. While we struggle to define literacy operationally (functional literacy, cultural literacy, computer literacy, etc.) and to predict which skills may be needed for success toward one's life goals (National Adult Literacy Survey, 2002), researchers agree on at least this one point: Lower literacy skills consistently result in a lower quality of life with fewer employment and leisure opportunities. Although adults bring a variety of formal educational experiences to the book club, they all want to learn. They all want to "talk" with friends, have a beverage, and tell each other about their week. The social context of the book club is paramount to adult learning. The social context that surrounds the NCBC—scheduling the meeting with their staff, going to a community meeting place, being an active participant during the book club, purchasing a beverage, and interacting with staff and customers in the café—all support adult-based learning. That's why our model emphasizes the intersections of social connection, literacy/learning, and community. For adults with ID to become members of literacy communities, we must consider reading and writing as socially constructed communicative practices, not as isolated skills to be practiced alone.

The National Institute for Literacy noted, "As the movement for independent living for persons with disabilities grows, the need for better and more competitive literacy skills also increases" (National Institute for Literacy, 1997). Though employers appear to be more willing to hire people with disabilities, employees need to have basic reading and interpersonal skills. Adults with ID continue to be both unemployed and underemployed at a disproportionate rate compared to other adults. For example, in Ohio, the successful closure ratio (getting a job) for a person with ID in the Vocational Rehabilitation system is 16 percent, while the successful closure ratio for all Vocational Rehabilitation consumers is 59 percent (Ohio Rehabilitation Services Commission, 2003). Providing opportunities for literacy learning directly addresses this disparity.

Access to literacy offers increased opportunities for inclusion into local community culture and is potentially a life-empowering event. The NCBC program provides this opportunity for adults with ID to continue to engage in literacy and social activities. At the same time, it helps to build necessary skills to obtain and maintain future employment opportunities. Several researchers have noted that book interactions, such as those the NCBC provides, are often highly motivating activities and an effective context for social interaction, communication, and literacy learning (Kirchner, 1991; Koppenhaver et al., 1991; Ratner et al., 1993; Watson et al., 1994). The expectation of the NCBC model is that members will continue to learn through participation in the club and will improve their sense of self-worth, because the program recognizes that they may be interested in and capable of learning.

We recognize that for some participants, independent literacy skills may not emerge. Historically, this has been an argument against inclusion of literacy activities for people with ID; that is, if conventional independent literacy is an unlikely outcome, then participating in literacy activities is illogical. We counter this claim by suggesting that participation in activities valued as part of our culture and human experience requires no definitive level of achievement to make the activity more or less rewarding or significant. Consider, for example, the value to the athletes, coaches, families, and spectators who participate in a Special Olympics competition. One could argue that the achievements of the Special Olympians, on a personal and social level, are every bit as significant as the world-record accomplishments of elite athletes. The magnitude of the achievement in terms of seconds and yards does not diminish the magnitude of the personal and social achievement for the competitors or the spectators. Similarly, we suggest that whether or not a member will become a conventional reader should not minimize the importance of interactive literacy activities (serving as the member's literacy partner and removing any barriers limiting this member's literacy participation). Participating in literacy at any level can improve quality of life, increase social interactions and relatedness, and improve communication skills. As one facilitator said, "You don't have to be able to read to enjoy a literary experience."

Both facilitators and members have realized increased reading ability and interest in reading. One member, Patty, is a forty-three-year-old woman who lives with her sister. After transporting Patty to and from her book club for six months, Patty's sister commented that she was amazed at how much more Patty had been reading since being in the NCBC. She noted that Patty was reading billboards and traffic signs as they drove to and from the book club, something she had never done before. Gary, a sixty-year-old man who had little formal educational experience, stated, "This is what I've wanted to do all my life: Since I've been in the book club, I've been learning."

> *Literacy does not merely mean being able to read. It also entails an understanding of the purpose of reading, the pleasure one experiences from reading, comprehending the stories, and being able to relate them to one's own life.*
> *—Nicole B, co-facilitator, Columbus, Ohio*

Literacy and ongoing adult education must be recognized as a basic human right for all people, with services starting at birth and continuing throughout life. The NCBC is an innovative program designed to integrate literacy and learning into social contexts for folks with a wide range of abilities. NCBC also seeks to empower members within their own communities, while increasing public awareness, self-esteem, and risk taking.

> *Shane is very high functioning and a good reader. He's an only child, and when we were new to the community, he joined the NCBC because he wanted a chance for more social interaction and to make friends.*
> *—Wanda S, parent and legal guardian, Hilliard, Ohio*

Social Connectedness

Similar to literacy, social connectedness—the extent to which people have friendships, engage in social activity, and feel a sense of belonging—positively correlates with a sense of empowerment and with overall quality of life (Lunsky & Neely, 2002). Interpersonal connections, friendships, and belonging play important roles in an individual's emotional and physical well-being. It is well recognized that our social activities help define us as people and promote self-esteem.

Similar to declines in literacy skills, participation in social activities, such as talking on the phone with friends and spending time with friends after work, also declines significantly for young adults with ID after they leave school (Wagner et al., 2004). Since the mid-1990s, individuals with ID have opportunities to participate in their communities in unprecedented numbers (Nisbet & Hagner, 2000); however, adults with ID often lack the social skills needed to participate in these events. The themes of social isolation and reduced support for people with ID recur in the literature (Lunsky & Neely, 2002; Pottie & Sumarah, 2004; Bramston et al., 2002; Chadsey & Beyer, 2001), regardless of family income or social background. Decreased support and fewer opportunities for activities result in a diminished quality of life.

> *Jeffrey was in assisted living since age fourteen in Port Clinton. Our parents died, then his roommate died, his case worker retired, and his care provider left town, so Jeff moved to Franklin County. He had no friends or peer relationships after moving here. Friendship Connection groups were 'cliquey.' Jeff joined the NCBC mainly for the social interaction; the reading was a bonus.*
> —Dean F, brother and co-facilitator, Blacklick, Ohio

NCBC members make social connections as part of their book club experience. Family members and facilitators report that the NCBC members have "made lasting friendships." These friendships often extend to the volunteer facilitators: "We have all become real friends and, to a great extent, have positively changed each other's lives" (Suzzanne F).

> *Stephanie is still in high school in a work program for social graduation. She works in the Sylvan Learning Center three hours a day pulling reading materials for classes. But she had lost contact with her friends, so she joined the NCBC mainly for the social skills.*
> —Stephen F, father, Westerville, Ohio

Community Inclusion

Evidence strongly indicates that a sense of social or community belonging correlates with overall quality of life. Research on the social isolation of people with ID routinely suggests increased leisure-time opportunities and utilization of the local resources as sources of support to address this isolation (O'Brien & O'Brien, 1993; Lunsky & Neely, 2002). However, despite our knowledge about the importance of connection to community, adults with ID continue to experience disproportionate segregation, isolation, and loneliness within their homes and communities (Bramston et al., 2002) and rarely participate in community activities, despite living and working in the community.

It's extremely important to be in the community doing what other people are doing, instead of just sitting at home, which can contribute to depression. The NCBC is pretty phenomenal…there are so few educational options after school ends.
—Peggy M, parent and legal guardian, Columbus, Ohio

To address these disparities, authentic community inclusion needs to extend beyond education and involve interacting and forming relationships with community members and belonging to clubs and organizations (Renzaglia et al., 2003). However, the research consistently suggests that these needs (of people with ID) are rarely identified or supported, and people with ID are in fact *not* regularly included as members of their communities (Nisbet & Hagner, 2000; Minnes et al., 2002). Local participation in community activities has also been significantly associated with improved social skills, positive affective demeanor, and increased levels of independence (Hunt et al., 1992). Other benefits of active local community participation for people with ID include increased economic productivity; improved health, well-being, and family functioning; higher life satisfaction; and more appropriate social interactions (Gracia & Herrero, 2004; Bramston et al., 2002). Adults with ID are more likely to experience success and build problem-solving skills if they are given the opportunity to apply skills in real-life community settings. In this natural community environment, social and literacy skills take on greater meaning (Renzaglia et al., 2003).

The NCBC model directly addresses many of the needs previously described. Clubs encourage the full inclusion of people in the cultural and social fabric of American society (Rehabilitation Act, 1973). They are held in community bookstores, cafés, and coffee shops—natural gathering places that have become increasingly popular in the last five years. People come to them to meet friends, buy a cup of coffee, do homework, read a book, and enjoy a variety of social activities.

People still go to bars to hang out and meet friends. Yet, the bookstore and coffee house scene may have a wider (and healthier) appeal to "come in and stay a while" without the pejorative connotation. (It's hard to imagine taking your laptop computer into a bar to check your email or reading a newspaper or magazine, without someone hounding you to buy a drink or order food. Similarly, you can go to Borders or Starbucks anytime of the day or night. Try going into a bar in the middle of the morning and see how people react.) People in bookstores and cafés can be productive or lazy or whatever they like. There's no expectation to be rowdy (like at a bar) or quiet (like at a library).

Local NCBC host sites provide an atmosphere in which members report feeling comfortable and included in typical adult activities. In these settings, staff and customers also meet and engage with NCBC members in natural contexts. Many members (and support staff) report pleasurable anticipation of NCBC meetings so that they might browse through the bookstore, select refreshments, and converse with host site customers and staff. As members become accustomed to their role as a contributing member of a neighborhood, they achieve greater community independence and rely less on facilitator support. Some members had never ordered their own drink before joining the NCBC, because it was always done for them.

She likes gathering at a grown-up place—Borders Café and Panera. She calls it 'going to her meeting.'
—Karen B, parent and legal guardian, Dublin, Ohio

Many NCBCs meet in central spaces within host sites, where public traffic is at its highest. One example is at Target stores, where the cafés are usually located right next to an entry/exit doorway. This exposure contributes to increased public awareness of people with ID and has elicited positive responses from customers. Several customers have approached the NCBC group and expressed interest in participating in the NCBC.

> *A young woman was at Espress Yourself Coffee House today when we began gathering for our book club. She shared that she had observed us several times in the past and liked what she saw. She is the owner of a dance studio, and we will be meeting to discuss her working with us as a volunteer theatre instructor, dance instructor, musical expression instructor, something. This is a great opportunity for us to be able to provide additional choices for our clients, and we have our participation in the book club to thank for this contact. It is amazing what the exposure to the community is bringing our way.*
> —*Jean T, former affiliate program coordinator and co-facilitator, Valparaiso, Indiana*

While the NCBC provides important opportunities for community inclusion, it represents only a beginning. The NCBC is merely a structured platform that allows people with disabilities to meet and participate in mainstream society. It is not spontaneous. We would like to see people with disabilities hanging out with their friends on their own and hope that will eventually happen with greater frequency. For now, however, such factors as dependence on others for transportation and limited experience initiating and maintaining friendships tend to curtail spontaneous activity.

For people with disabilities, community inclusion means more than simply living in the community. It should translate to going wherever one wants, whenever one wants to go there. Figure 3 illustrates the critical success factors for people with disabilities engaging in community activities.

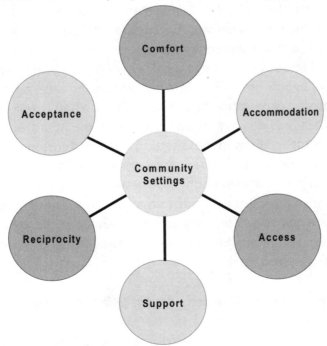

Figure 3—Critical success factors for people with disabilities engaging in community activities

To create opportunities for people with disabilities to engage meaningfully in community activities, the Next Chapter Book Club depends on the following factors and strives to enhance them in community settings:

- Comfort: attractive, friendly, and relaxed environment
- Accommodation: interaction with host site staff to meet members' needs
- Access: physical facility and transportation to meeting locations
- Support: developing friendships with other members and facilitators
- Reciprocity: members and facilitators helping themselves and each other
- Acceptance: by other members, facilitators, host site staff, and customers

Reciprocal Relationships in the NCBC Model

Figure 4—The Next Chapter Book Club model

The Next Chapter Book Club is effective because of the reciprocal relationships among its three major components. As literacy and learning facilitate interactions with others, they also broaden exploration of one's community. Social interactions and social connectedness significantly enhance literacy and learning, and are essential components of a vibrant community life. Active community participation and community inclusion foster the retention of literacy and social skills as well as social learning. Like the three legs of a stool, no one component is more important than the others.

I really like this place a lot, with the friends, the book, and the drink!
—Van, member, Columbus, Ohio

3 Who Are NCBC Affiliates?

An affiliate is not a member, a facilitator, or a host site. It is also not a contributor, such as a foundation or Rotary Club, that provides financial support to the NCBC. Affiliates may be literacy groups, disability agencies, parent organizations, service agencies, libraries, and/or private individuals. Virtually any organization or individual can sponsor an NCBC program in their community. Affiliates take primary responsibility for organizing all book club activities at the local level.

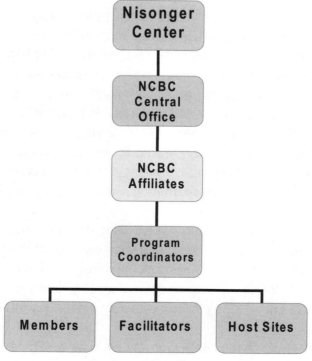

Figure 5—NCBC Affiliates

Often an agency will collaborate with other community groups to form an affiliate, sponsor the training workshop from the NCBC Central Office, and conduct local activities. In such cases, one organization is usually the main point of contact for the affiliate.

An affiliate arranges for the training workshop just mentioned, which is intended for both program coordinators and facilitators. (See Chapter 4 for details about affiliate training workshops.) Affiliate staff, usually the program coordinator, is responsible for the ongoing aspects of running the program, including the following (see also Chapter 5 for details):

- member and facilitator recruitment and screening;
- facilitator training;
- arranging host site locations and talking with store managers to explain NCBC; and
- monitoring clubs on a regular basis.

Affiliate organizations tend to be those that are passionate about community inclusion and recognize the importance of socialization and lifelong learning for adults with ID. They also are risk takers, creative, and forward-thinking. Without exception, one individual within an affiliate organization is willing to take a leap of faith and advocate operating a book club. In some cases it takes time for these visionaries to convince others in their community to support their efforts philosophically and financially. Let's take a look at just a few of these hardy souls and the organizations they represent.

Profiles of NCBC Affiliates

Jean Tarquinio, Valparaiso, Indiana

Ms. Jean Tarquinio worked for Opportunity Enterprises, Inc., an agency serving the MR/DD population in Valparaiso, for twenty-two years. She wrote to us in November 2005 after reading about the NCBC in a *Disability Solutions* article. Her letter said, "We would like to be an affiliate agency with me as the facilitator and coordinator of the program. Over the past year I have brought Best Buddies, Self Advocacy, and SibShops to our agency, and I believe NCBC might be a challenge worth undertaking." We sent the information she requested about training costs, and then did not hear from her for several months. In March 2006 we sent our new training flyer and learned that, due to funding issues, they were not starting new projects that wouldn't produce revenue. Jean said, "We believe the program would be a great asset to our special projects, just not right at this moment. You remain on my radar." We suggested that she consider partnering with another agency in her area to co-sponsor the training and share costs.

And partner she did! To our pleasant surprise, we heard from Jean in June 2006 that her proposal for the NCBC had been approved. In October of that year we conducted a training for agencies providing residential, educational, advocacy, and vocational support for people with disabilities in seven Indiana communities on the same day: Crown Point, Gary, Highland, Hobart, Michigan City, Rolling Prairie, and Valparaiso. All are now NCBC affiliates with active clubs, as well as another in Ft. Wayne.

Today was another Next Chapter Book Club day. While we were meeting, a gentleman came in and sat behind our group. As I was preparing to leave, the gentleman said, qui-

Ben Mikaelsen, author of *Touching Spirit Bear*, met with members of Opportunity Enterprises' NCBC in Valparaiso, Indiana. They read the book together as part of the Valpo Reads A Book program in April 2007. Photo © 2007, Sun-Times News Group.

etly, *'That was the most noble thing I have watched in years.' We then discussed what had actually happened and his view of our book club. He was so struck by the simplicity of what he watched and the importance of it. I invited this gentleman back to join us and read with us. He hopes, as do I, that he will find the time to do that; for him, this was an amazing moment.*

We see amazing moments every day and at times scurry right past them in our hurry to get the job done. I, however, feel the 'special-ness' of this book club each Monday. Aren't I a lucky girl? Come join us and read with us for an hour; it is like a breath of fresh air on a crisp fall morning.

—Jean T, former affiliate program coordinator and co-facilitator, Valparaiso, Indiana

Jack Snook, Pittsburgh, Pennsylvania

Mr. Jack Snook is a program director at the United Cerebral Palsy of Pittsburgh and liked the idea of NCBC from the very beginning. Yet he realized that operating a book club program would require increasing the visibility of his agency and partnering with other disability organizations in the greater Pittsburgh area to defray the training costs. This process took several months to accomplish. Jack said at times it was like taking one step forward and two steps back. Like with any new and unproven initiative, Jack ran into several roadblocks along the way.

However, his perseverance paid off. His UCP organization collaborated with the Down Syndrome Association of Pittsburgh to pay the workshop fee. Jack and Susan Cataldi, a life skills teacher from Fox Chapel, coordinated a training workshop that Tom Fish conducted for eighteen people in early 2007. Jack said, "It was great—we received a lot of positive feedback." The people attending the training were largely from the Pittsburgh area, including two representatives from the local YMCA, but also from the Johnstown area and Greensburg-Westmoreland County. Jack sent us this update on the clubs that were in progress as of April 2007:

> I just wanted you to know that the group from Westmoreland County that attended the training has one group up and running and one on the way. The group that is currently going has six men, and they are reading 'Charlie and the Chocolate Factory.' One group member has minimal reading skills; the others cannot read at all. Tara B is the facilitator and she has a volunteer from St. Vincent's College assisting her. She is working on establishing a women's group in the local college coffee shop, and recruiting a volunteer from the Murraysville area. So they are moving right along.
> —Jack S, affiliate program coordinator, Pittsburgh, Pennsylvania

Eddie Tebbe, New Orleans, Louisiana

Mr. Eddie Tebbe was responsible for bringing the NCBC to New Orleans. Mr. Tebbe, who has cerebral palsy, is the transition specialist for Families Helping Families of Greater New Orleans, Inc. According to Eddie, the NCBC model "made a lot of sense to me. . . . It embodies what I've always done in my life, which is to fully participate in the community."

Eddie has worked at Families Helping Families for over a year and loves his job. He talks about having been trained as a teacher at the University of New Orleans, but says that he prefers working in the community helping people with disabilities become more aware and self-confident. His book club meets in Barnes & Noble, and his sister and friends serve as co-facilitators.

Other Louisiana branches of Families Helping Families operate NCBCs in Harahan, Lafayette, Lake Charles, Monroe, and Shreveport.

Sue Neal, Mansfield, Ohio

Ms. Sue Neal is a support specialist with the Richland County Board of MR/DD in Mansfield, Ohio. She has worked for the county board for twenty-five years. Sue learned about NCBC from her boss, the agency director, who liked the idea and asked Sue to follow up and take a lead role in bringing NCBC to Mansfield. Within a year and a half, Sue established three clubs and will soon have another starting. Two clubs meet at a Barnes & Noble and one meets at a local restaurant called The Upper Crust (which happens to be owned by the parent of someone in Sue's program).

According to Sue, most of her volunteers are retired and wouldn't miss coming to their club except for bad weather. One of them, a woman in her eighties, said to Sue, "This is one of the most rewarding things I've done in my life." Sue notes that for her personally, the most rewarding aspect about the NCBC has been the response from patrons. She says that all kinds of people come over and inquire about what books the clubs are reading and comment on the clubs. Every week at The Upper Crust, the same policeman is there having a cup of coffee. He always stops by and says to the club members, "I really enjoyed seeing you guys today."

Sue says, "The book clubs are a good experience for everyone concerned." She is a straightforward individual who is not afraid to speak her mind. "I don't do things I don't enjoy doing." Sue has tremendous compassion and the ability to look creatively at how to help people with ID.

> *You must be very proud of all the growth of your book clubs. It seems as if once people hear about it they are sold. Everyone likes to be involved. I know people at our host sites are always stopping by to tell us how much they enjoy having us there. They seem amazed at how much fun we have. I think they stop by to see if the happy rubs off. It seems that most everyone has some kind of story to tell about our group or someone they know who is involved with a reading group. If we happen to miss a day due to bad weather or a holiday, the next time we are there people always come in and say, 'Boy, we're glad you came back.' We just have a lot of fun. Thanks for turning us on!!!*
> —Sue N, affiliate program coordinator, Mansfield, Ohio

Current NCBC Affiliates

- The Ability Center, Port Clinton/Oak Harbor, Ohio
- AmeriCorps Programs
- Anthis Career Center, Ft. Wayne, Indiana
- Arc BRIDGES in several Indiana communities
- Boonton Holmes Public Library, Boonton, New Jersey
- Community Connections, Association for the Developmentally Disabled
- County Boards of MR/DD in several Ohio counties
- DAWN Center for Independent Living, Inc., Sparta and Rockaway, New Jersey
- Down Syndrome Association of Roanoke, Virginia
- Down Syndrome Research Foundation, Burnaby, British Columbia, Canada
- Down Syndrome Society of Rhode Island, Cranston, Rhode Island
- Fairfax County Public Schools, Fairfax County, Virginia
- Families Helping Families in several Louisiana communities
- Hattie's Cafe & Gifts (Hattie Larlham), Akron/Hudson, Ohio
- Hope Homes, Inc., Stow, Ohio
- Hopewell Industries, Coshocton, Ohio
- Jewish Services for the Developmentally Disabled, West Orange, New Jersey
- Michiana Resources, Inc., Michigan City, Indiana
- Milwaukee Center For Independence, Milwaukee, Wisconsin
- The Ohio State University Nisonger Center, Columbus, Ohio
- Opportunity Enterprises, Inc., Valparaiso, Indiana
- Roxbury Parents for Exceptional Children, Inc., Roxbury Township, New Jersey
- SAGE at Goodwill Industries, Columbus, Ohio
- Saratoga Bridges, Saratoga Springs, New York
- Scotch Plains Public Library, Scotch Plains, New Jersey
- Share Foundation, Rolling Prairie, Indiana

Joy and Robert (back row, center) from Down Syndrome Research Foundation in Burnaby, British Columbia, visit a book club in Columbus, Ohio. The DSRF operates book clubs and is responsible for training other affiliates in Canada.

- Speech and Language Pathologists
- Southbay Mental Health, Boston, Massachusetts
- Starlight Enterprises, Inc., New Philadelphia, Ohio
- Teachers and Transition Coordinators
- Therapy & Alternatives for Special Children and Adults, Fort Erie, Ontario, Canada
- Thousand Oaks Public Library, Thousand Oaks, California
- United Cerebral Palsy (UCP) of Pittsburgh, Pennsylvania
- University of Cologne, Germany
- University of Illinois, RSA Region V CRP-RCEP
- University of Missouri-St. Louis
- Upreach (Learning Never Ends), Columbus, Ohio
- UPS for DownS, Chicago, Illinois
- WorkNet, Marysville, Ohio

4 What Happens at an NCBC Affiliate Training Workshop?

Our book club in Sparta, New Jersey, at Panera Bread is really going great. The response has been so overwhelming that I had to start a second night. I am holding a training for two teachers from the local high schools in mid-November to become facilitators. I am going to use the PowerPoint® and instructor's guide to train. They have expressed interest in taking over the Monday night at Sparta. I am currently working on starting one at a Panera Bread in Hackettstown, N.J., after the first of the year. All of you out in Ohio have created an amazing program that is having such a positive impact on so many young people's lives. I can't thank you enough and I will continue to make sure that each club is run with all the Next Chapter's guidelines, activities, and goals being met.

—Sean H, affiliate program coordinator and co-facilitator, Sparta, New Jersey

From 2002 until the time of this book's printing, the Next Chapter Book Club has grown from two pilot clubs in Columbus, Ohio, to over 130 book clubs in fifteen states and three countries. Presentations at local and national conferences, published articles, and word-of-mouth continue to attract individuals and organizations who wish to join the NCBC family.

Just as the program itself has evolved, the NCBC affiliate training has evolved into a five- to six-hour workshop that includes an overview of the NCBC model; the history and rationale for the development of the NCBC; and suggested strategies, activities, and tools to use in book clubs. The workshop also includes a demonstration book club that gives workshop participants a first-hand look at the NCBC in action. The objectives of the affiliate training workshops are that participants will

- gain a thorough understanding of the Next Chapter Book Club (NCBC) model and philosophy;
- learn how to promote literacy and lifelong learning opportunities for adolescents and adults with intellectual disabilities;

- learn how to optimize social and community experiences for adolescents and adults with intellectual disabilities; and
- acquire the knowledge and tools necessary to operate an NCBC program in their community.

Getting Started

Organizations, groups, or individuals who participate in training workshops typically include local or statewide disability service providers, disability advocacy organizations, transition programs, schools, libraries, parents or family members of people with ID. These affiliates are then responsible for coordinating the program on an ongoing basis at the local level. Tasks of the program coordinator include recruitment, monitoring, and overall program implementation and are described in more detail in Chapter 5.

We hold the training workshop in the affiliate's community. Workshop participants include staff from the affiliate organization and people from other disability, literacy, and community service programs who may wish to participate, as well as people with ID. We have found that it works quite well for several local organizations to collaborate, share costs, and receive training at the same time. These organizations may be from the local area or other communities. For example, in 2007 we trained representatives from five disability organizations throughout Louisiana in one session and in one location, and each one now operates a Next Chapter Book Club.

The NCBC Central Office corresponds with the prospective affiliate and provides resources including a pre-workshop checklist to help to prepare for all aspects of the training. Once the training workshop is scheduled, NCBC staff guides and supports the affiliate staff through arrangements for the upcoming workshop. Since the training workshop takes place in the affiliate's community, staff in the affiliate organization or collaborating agencies complete the majority of tasks. However, NCBC training staff often assists by providing information, resources, and suggestions during this process. Preparing for the workshop involves the tasks described in the rest of this section.

Identifying the Location of the Training

The first part of the training workshop involves an interactive slide presentation and is often held at the affiliate agency or in a library or other meeting room. The trainer from the NCBC Central Office brings all necessary equipment, materials, and handouts. We ask affiliates to select a training location conducive to a slide presentation, with an electrical outlet and a screen or blank wall upon which to project the slides. The room should be large enough to accommodate the number of participants expected. We also advise affiliates to consider availability of parking and accessibility of the training room. For example, if the training is to be held in a second floor room, is there an elevator for participants who may not be able to climb stairs? When two or more agencies join together for one training workshop, often the agency that has taken the lead in coordinating the training, or the one with the most central location, will host the training.

Inviting Workshop Participants and Getting the Word Out

Participants can be people from the affiliate organization and any other organization or community group who would like to collaborate on the project. We have presented our workshops to groups of five to thirty-five people, and there is no maximum number of participants. Depending on the intended size and scope of the local program, affiliates may choose to limit the training workshop to employees of that agency. Some affiliates may invite other agencies, libraries, schools and universities, and/or literacy organizations to become collaborators. Many affiliates open the training workshop beyond their professional circle to the community-at-large.

Once an affiliate determines who will be invited, they often issue informal invitations verbally or through email. NCBC Central Office provides affiliates with a flyer template to publicize the upcoming training workshop. Affiliates often customize this flyer and post it in strategic locations such as agency break rooms, libraries, bookstores, coffee shops, and universities. Some affiliates also use advertisements in agency newsletters and more formal written invitations. So that the NCBC trainer may prepare the appropriate amount of training materials, we ask that affiliates provide us with a headcount prior to the workshop. Therefore, we suggest that flyers and invitations include instructions to register for the workshop.

Soliciting Demonstration Book Club Participants

The second portion of the workshop includes a forty- to fifty-minute demonstration of the NCBC model. The NCBC Central Office trainer facilitates this "demo." Affiliates recruit five or six adolescents and/or adults with disabilities to participate in this demonstration book club. Recruiting strategies for demo participants can vary depending on the nature of the affiliate organization. For example, a disability service provider will have a more accessible recruiting pool than a public library that serves the general community. To recruit demo participants, as well as ongoing book club members, affiliates that are not directly connected with a group of potential NCBC members must reach out to local agencies or individuals who are.

Demo participants are usually recruited in person, through individual invitations, or announcements during meetings or activities. Flyers can also be used to advertise the opportunity to participate in the demonstration; however affiliates must be mindful that this does not exclude potential participants who do not read without support. We reiterate at this time that book club members can have a range of literacy skills from readers to "emergent" readers and anywhere in between. We welcome demonstration participants to take part in the entire training workshop if they wish.

Recruiting Volunteer Facilitators

Trained volunteer facilitators typically lead Next Chapter Book Clubs. (See Chapter 8, "Who Are NCBC Facilitators?" and Chapter 9, "What Do NCBC Facilitators Do?" for details.) Affiliates recruit volunteer facilitators by posting announcements to listservs, advertising in local publications, and word-of-mouth, among other methods. (See the "Recruiting" section of Chapter 5 for more details.) We also discuss general and community-specific volunteer recruitment strategies during the training workshop.

If affiliates have identified volunteer facilitators prior to the workshop, we encourage them to attend so they can learn all they can about the NCBC and participate in the demonstration. If no facilitators have volunteered for the position prior to the workshop, often the NCBC trainer and one of the workshop participants will co-facilitate the demonstration club. By the time the workshop is over, affiliate program coordinators are equipped to train future volunteers with the knowledge gained during the workshop as well as a resource CD that includes a facilitator training presentation.

Identifying a Community Host Site for the Demonstration

After the presentation portion of the training, the participants move from the training location to a community setting to demonstrate the NCBC model. Affiliates should choose a site ahead of time where demo participants are free to socialize and have an opportunity to interact with the community around them. Most often, these are public gathering places such as bookstores, cafés (not sit-down restaurants), and coffee shops. (See "Finding Host Sites" in Chapter 5 and "How Do I Select a Host Site?" in Chapter 10 for details.) For purposes of the demonstration, affiliates should select a site with enough room for the demo participants as well as those observing. Avoid peak business hours when possible.

Once the affiliate staff identifies an appropriate site for the demonstration, we recommend that she notify the site manager about the NCBC and the demonstration planned in their facility. It may be helpful to give the manager a copy of the workshop flyer mentioned above. Although it is not necessary to ask for permission to meet in a public place, host sites can be valuable allies, and it's best to establish a positive relationship from the start. (See "How Should I Approach a Host Site Manager?" in Chapter 10.) The manager may be able to reserve a table(s) for the demonstration, which may be imperative if the group is very large. In some cases, when the size of the group at the demonstration is too large, it may be necessary to conduct the demo group at the training site rather than in a community host site.

Selecting Books for the Demonstration

Demo group participants may choose which book they would like to read during the workshop demonstration. Prior to the workshop, the NCBC trainer sends to the affiliate staff a list of available books from which the demo participants choose, or they may request a book that is not on the list. It's helpful if they rank their top three choices. NCBC Central Office delivers to the affiliate the set of books participants have chosen.

The Affiliate Training Workshop

Fees

The usual fee for a day-long affiliate training workshop is $1,000 plus travel expenses (transportation, meals, and lodging) for one trainer from the NCBC Central Office. Included in this price are all the materials for participants, including a set of books for the first book club. For affiliates in Ohio, we offer a discounted in-state fee of $600 plus minimal travel expenses.

Sample Schedule

A typical affiliate training workshop schedule is below; however, no two training workshops look the same. We will make adjustments in the workshop schedule to accommodate an affiliate's time and logistical constraints.

Table 2.   Sample schedule for NCBC affiliate training workshop

9:00 – 9:20 AM	Introductions
9:20 – 10:30 AM	Interactive slide presentation and discussion
10:30 – 10:40 AM	Break
10:40 AM – 12:00 PM	Presentation and discussion continued
12:00 – 1:00 PM	Lunch and move to community host site for demonstration
1:00 – 1:40 PM	Demonstration book club
1:40 – 2:00 PM	Discussion of demo
2:00 – 2:30 PM	Action plan, evaluations, and final comments

The first half of the workshop day involves an interactive presentation that includes instruction, discussion, and small-group work. Topics covered are as follows:
- history and rationale for the development of the NCBC;
- description of members, facilitators, and host sites;
- overview of the NCBC model;
- suggested facilitation strategies and book club activities;
- steps involved in getting a book club off the ground, including tips for recruiting and supporting volunteers; and
- ongoing program coordination and management considerations.

The Demonstration

After the training presentation, workshop participants break for lunch and then re-group at the community host site for the demonstration book club. Often the NCBC trainer will invite one of the workshop participants to co-facilitate the demonstration club. The demo typically starts with introductions, a brief description of the NCBC, and the reason for the group of people surrounding and observing the club. (This is helpful, because most of the demo participants have probably not been to the first part of the workshop.) Because this is almost always a novel experience for the demo participants, there is often hesitation among some to join in the conversation and reading. (It is advisable to limit the demo audience to perhaps a dozen people, as a large group can be both distracting and intimidating to demo participants.) However, after observing others joining in and having fun, even the quietest participants get involved. Since this is the first book club meeting, it is usually necessary for the trainer to be more directive than is optimal. As is explained during the workshop, the need for facilitator intervention tends to fade as book club members become comfortable and accustomed to the activity.

Jillian Ober from the NCBC Central Office conducts a demonstration book club in Roanoke, Virginia.

Feedback From Workshop Participants

"Your presentation was helpful and very informative. After some apprehension at first, I am really looking forward and excited about getting our book club started."
—New Philadelphia, Ohio

"The demonstration with the consumers was amazing. This group of consumers was meeting for the first time with a new focus—the book club. This was unlike any other experience offered at Milwaukee Center for Independence (MCFI). They were attentive, interested, and appeared to be enjoying the book."
—Milwaukee, Wisconsin

"I learned a lot. I had questions to ask but the trainer answered them before I had to ask. It was very informative and the demonstration was great!"
—Toledo, Ohio

"I enjoyed the training and found the various ideas for games and activities useful."
—Roanoke, Virginia

"The demonstration was truly enlightening!"
—Toledo, Ohio

(Regarding the demonstration): "I did not know Jared read so well. And to see him truly laugh ...!"
—Lafayette, Louisiana

"We feel like we're ready to get started!"
—Saratoga, New York

How Do Local Program Coordinators Run an NCBC Program?

5

Just a note to let you know that Next Chapter Tucson continues to rock ... six members, four facilitators, and one student from the speech, language, and hearing department at the University of Arizona interning with us. Nothing to sneeze at.

—Fran M, affiliate program coordinator, Tucson, Arizona

The program coordinator (PC) is responsible for the daily maintenance of the NCBC program as well as local program development and expansion. Key activities for which the PC is responsible are recruiting facilitators and members, training and monitoring the volunteer facilitators, overall program coordination including monitoring and evaluation, maintaining the library of books, and communicating with host sites.

Who Can Be a Program Coordinator?

A program coordinator is usually an employee of the affiliate organization. Affiliates take primary responsibility for organizing all book club activities at the local level. If not an affiliate staff member, a PC can just as easily be one of the following:

- a parent or a person with a disability;
- a disability services agency staff member;
- a library or literacy organization staff member; or
- any community member with an interest in promoting literacy, social connectedness, and community inclusion for people with disabilities.

An ideal PC will have strong organization and communication skills (oral and written) and preferably will also have experience working with adolescents and/or adults with ID. An effective PC will also be resourceful, creative, and enthusiastic. Depending on size of the local program, the PC can expect to devote from two to twenty hours on the project weekly.

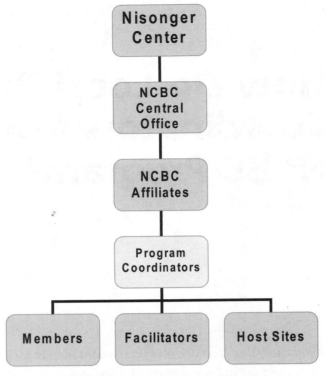

Figure 6—NCBC Program Coordinators

Recruiting

Recruiting NCBC members and facilitators is a primary and ongoing responsibility of the PC. Member recruiting may occur through a variety of activities, such as

- presentations to people with ID at places of employment or at schools;
- presentations to supported living providers or others who have contact with people with ID; and
- networking with local service provider agencies and within the larger community.

Our recruitment goal is to develop a variety of broad-based community public service venues that will provide to their members ongoing contact information regarding participation in the NCBC.

For those unsure about joining a book club, the PC presents the NCBC as a chance to make new friends, learn and hang out in a fun, community place. People who cannot read or who have had negative experiences with reading in the past may be especially hesitant to join a book club. In this case, the PC assures them that the NCBC is a safe and accepting place. He may say something like this:

> Many people in our book clubs have trouble reading, and many don't read at all. So you won't be the only one who might feel a little nervous. There are people at each book club who are there to help and encourage you. Besides, the book club is about much more than reading! It's a chance to make friends, learn new things, and get out and have fun in a coffee shop or bookstore.

Once a potential member (or family member or support staff) has expressed interest in the NCBC, the PC provides him with a "Member Intake Form" to be completed and returned (Appendix B). The Member Intake Form provides much of the demographic information the PC needs to organize an NCBC and also includes a photo and video release. The PC informs members and their family or support staff, as appropriate, that they are responsible for making every effort to come to book club each week and behave appropriately while there. (See Frequently Asked Questions.) Many members enjoy purchasing their own beverage or refreshments during the club meeting. The PC reminds the member that he needs to bring money to the NCBC if he wants to buy something.

Next Chapter Book Club
Member Intake Form

1. What is your name?
2. How old are you?
3. What is your phone number? ___ Birthdate?
4. What is your address?
5. Do you live alone? Do you live with family or roomma
6. What days and times are you available to participate i
7. What kind of books would you like to read?
8. Are there things you shouldn't eat or drink? Do you ha (ex. seizures) or special needs we should know about

Appendix B *(p. 165)*

We recruit facilitators through a variety of paper, electronic, and personal outreach strategies. The PC may distribute brochures and/or post flyers at bookstores, coffee shops, student unions, places of worship, and on community bulletin boards. He may also electronically post facilitator recruitment information to disability and university department listservs. Presenting at service provider and supported living agencies and other social service organizations has also resulted in recruitment of facilitator volunteers. One of the most successful strategies for recruiting facilitators is word of mouth; so seize opportunities to spread the word in your community.

When recruiting potential facilitators, the PC describes the fundamental aspects of the program and how participation can be a fulfilling, and even life-changing, experience for volunteers. Facilitating an NCBC offers volunteer facilitators an opportunity to provide direct service and the ability to see first-hand how their efforts affect the book club members. (See Chapters 8 and 9 for more information on the role of volunteer facilitators.) We encourage NCBC facilitators and members to be inventive and flexible to create the kind of book club they would like to have. Lastly, facilitating an NCBC is a chance to volunteer for a short amount of time; few volunteer opportunities require only about an hour per week.

The PC creates and maintains a program database that includes member and facilitator demographic information, such as name, contact information, age, and length of time in the NCBC. The database enables the affiliate to monitor the progress of the clubs, describe the characteristics of the members and facilitators, and observe trends over time. This helps with future recruitment, program planning, and fund-raising.

Training

Before we train a potential facilitator, we recommend that he visit an NCBC to observe the activity. The volunteer can then make an informed decision about the suitability of the NCBC and discuss his experience during training. We also recommend that any PC who did not observe a demonstration book club during the training workshop visit an active NCBC.

The PC ensures compliance with his agency policies on liability and background screening for volunteers. Because NCBC facilitators are working with a vulnerable population, we recommend background checks for all volunteers. If the affiliate is an individual not employed by an agency, then he is responsible for conducting background checks and securing liability insurance coverage. If the PC works for an agency, it is likely he has already had a background check. If he does not work for an agency and is not facilitating a club, he does not need one. If an affiliate does not have the capability to conduct its own background checks, it may be possible to collaborate with a state or local service provider or other agency that can do them.

Training for new facilitators typically requires sixty to ninety minutes with the PC. We adapt the training to each volunteer but always include the following activities:

- in-depth overview of the training manual content and Facilitator Position Description (Appendix D);
- discussion on confidentiality, consumer rights, and responsibilities;
- completion of the Facilitator Intake Form (Appendix C); and
- answering any questions and concerns.

The PC may schedule additional training sessions as requested or needed.

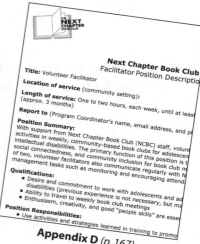

Appendix D (p. 167)

Retention

Retaining volunteer facilitators largely depends on how supported and valued they feel. To that end, the PC visits each book club approximately every month or two to observe and provide feedback on the facilitator's performance, share tips and approaches, and offer other assistance as needed. In addition to the feedback received at book club visits, the PC gains valuable information through the Monthly Facilitator Report that facilitators complete on the NCBC website to summarize the members' attendance and progress. Also, the PC periodically contacts facilitators to solicit feedback and offer assistance on any issues or ideas discussed. The PC fosters a good relationship with facilitators through regular positive reinforcement and occasional tokens of appreciation, such as a gift card paid for by the affiliate. Despite these efforts, circumstances may cause facilitators to vacate their position. When a club needs a new facilitator, the PC repeats the recruitment and training steps described above. To avoid putting a club on hiatus, he might need to fill in until the position is filled. He also attends the new facilitator's first club meeting to encourage a smooth transition.

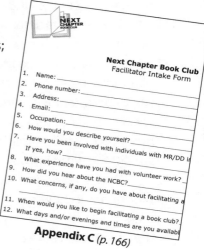

Appendix C (p. 166)

Scheduling

The PC forms a new club based on interest and availability of members matched with two volunteer facilitators. It's often best for the co-facilitators (in concert with the PC) to decide on a day, time, and location before recruiting members. Trying to match each member's schedule beforehand may be impossible. Once these details are coordinated, the PC verifies that each member has reliable transportation to and from the club. The PC then provides facilitators with a list of members' names and phone numbers. As a courtesy, the PC also contacts the host site before the first meeting to inform them of the NCBC meeting day and time. (See the "Finding Host Sites" section later in this chapter.)

Because NCBCs are open groups, membership may change over time. The average length of stay is about one year, though many of our members have stayed longer. When a new member is added to a club, the PC informs the facilitators and updates all records. Likewise, when a member leaves a club, the PC updates records and also contacts the former member to understand the reason for leaving. When the number of people interested in joining book clubs exceeds the number of available slots, the PC forms a waiting list and contacts the people on it regularly to apprise them of their status. If there are enough prospective members to form a new club, then the PC recruits and trains volunteer facilitators and host sites as before.

Monitoring, Support, and Evaluation

Program monitoring is an ongoing activity. The PC or another affiliate staff person visits each club about once a month to meet and talk with members and facilitators and to model any new strategies or activities. The club visits serve several purposes: 1) to ensure member and facilitator satisfaction, 2) to address minor concerns, 3) to assure ongoing quality activities are taking place, and 4) to collect information regarding the effectiveness of each club. With input from the facilitators, the PC collects information on changes in members' literacy and social skills through the completion of the Five-Level Scale of Literacy Skills (Appendix H) or the ECO-NCBC Literacy Observations (Appendix I) forms. Administering these forms before the club starts and again about six to nine months later will help to document progress for the members, facilitators, affiliates, and program sponsors.

Facilitators log on to a secure page on the NCBC website to submit their Monthly Facilitator Report (Appendix E). The PC shares this information with the pro-

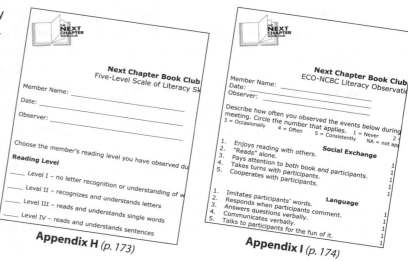

Appendix H (p. 173)   **Appendix I** (p. 174)

gram director (or affiliate agency director) and the Advisory Board to continuously improve the program's effectiveness.

When a group completes a book, the PC should consider administering the Member End-of-Book Survey (Appendix F) and issue certificates of completion or accomplishment to members and facilitators (Appendix G).

Josh had a lot of trouble staying awake and didn't seem very involved in the reading or the discussion of 'The Story of Dr. Dolittle.' When it was Josh's turn to read, Cindy, the facilitator, started reading long phrases of four or five words for him to echo. He would barely say the last word in each phrase. Picking up on that, Cindy shortened to two-word phrases, many of which he still skipped to the last word. She needed to repeat and prod him constantly.

At one point, when Cindy said a phrase, Josh looked at the book and instead of echoing, read the next three words in the sentence! I waited for a pause and then gently suggested that Cindy let Josh try a word first, and only help him on the ones he doesn't know. When he didn't know the next three words, I thought my plan might have backfired. But, before the paragraph was completed, Josh had read several sentences completely by himself, including a long word like 'strawberry'! When I praised him for his accomplishment, his smile was as wide as his face. Then when Cindy was asking background questions about events in earlier chapters, Josh seemed to remember more details than the other members.

When the session was wrapping up, I asked Josh if he knew he could read so many words. He smiled shyly and said, 'No.' Then Cindy said that was the first time he had read, and she didn't know he could read at all! So I took that as a training opportunity and reinforced the idea that we need to give members a chance to read whatever they can. Cindy took it well and appreciated my help.

—*Vicki G, program manager, Columbus, Ohio*

Book and Supply Inventory

The NCBC local affiliate receives a starter set of books from the NCBC Central Office at the training workshop. After that, the affiliate may obtain books through donations, public libraries, and/or foundation funding as available. The PC obtains multiple copies of each book, so that each member may borrow a copy and take it home while the group is reading the book. The cost averages about $5.00 per copy; quantity discounts are often available. Depending on how books are obtained, affiliates may decide to give them to members when each book is completed. If the affiliate is operating more than one club, it may choose to keep a central library for lending books on a rotating basis. Maintaining an updated inventory of books in the NCBC library is critical as the number of clubs expands. Accurate recording of which club is reading which book will save much time as clubs complete books and look for new ones to read. The PC is also responsible for ordering and distributing any other (optional) supplies used in the program, such as book bags, T-shirts, brochures, pens, markers, dry erase boards, bookmarks, and other promotional materials.

When a club is ready for a new book, the PC provides the facilitators with a list and descriptions of currently available books and asks facilitators to respond with the members' top three choices. The PC then exchanges books during a club visit or through other arrangements. If a member wishes to purchase a book from the lending library, the PC can decide on a fair price, based on the book's age and condition. The PC would then need to replace it. Another option is for members to purchase their own books (perhaps from the very bookstore where they meet) and affiliates to provide them for facilitators. We strongly recommend this option, so that members are able to establish a personal library, demonstrate their commitment to the club, and promote self-determination.

> *I felt that the members were able to peak in their reading when the type of books we read sparked their interest because they had pictures, large print, and a simple storyline, which, when they returned to a week later, was not forgotten. 'Harry Potter' was definitely a long and winding read for the members, and they became bored with it sometimes.*
> *—Amber M, co-facilitator, Gahanna, Ohio*

Making Book Accommodations

If a member requires some form of accommodation to participate in the activity (such as a large print or Braille book, sign language interpretation, etc.), the PC works with the member and his family or support staff, if appropriate, to make those arrangements. Many states have libraries for the blind that can provide Braille books or books on tape to people with visual impairments. The Library of Congress will do this also. State ADA offices may also be able to assist in providing accommodations. See also the Resources section of this book.

Some book accommodations pose challenges for facilitators. For example, members of one Columbus club were all students at the Ohio State School for the Blind (OSSB). The first book they selected was *Around the World in 80 Days*. Some shared an original edition in Braille, borrowed from the state library; some read an adapted classics edition in large print; and some read an electronic edition that could be accessed on their Braille notes machines. All three versions of the text were different! As each member took a turn reading, the facilitators encouraged other members to follow along when they could, and just to listen and enjoy the story when they couldn't. The challenge was in determining where the page breaks in the Braille version corresponded to the page breaks in other editions. Hillary J, the co-facilitator, said, "Next time, we'll definitely try to make sure at least two versions of the book are the same!"

Blind students use large print and Braille notes machines during club meetings.

Stacy's only limitation is a serious vision impairment; she uses large print and a magnifying glass. She's more willing to try to do things on her own since joining the NCBC, such as writing cards and letters to people.

—Carol C, grandparent and legal guardian, Gahanna, Ohio

Finding Host Sites

Primary considerations when searching for a host site include places that offer refreshments and places that provide opportunities for group interaction and socializing. Most often in our community, these are neighborhood bookstores, coffee shops, or cafés. We do not recommend restaurants with sit-down service due to the distraction of ordering food.

The PC checks to be sure that the host site is in a safe location and is accessible. For those who use wheelchairs, meeting in a location with portable tables and chairs is helpful. Locations near public transportation are preferred. The PC cultivates a relationship with host site employees through periodic visits and is available to address any concerns that may develop. (For more detailed discussion of potential host sites and how to approach host site managers, see Chapter 10.)

Community Collaborations and Program Development

Another activity of the PC is to identify and contact local disability and literacy groups for possible collaboration and program expansion. Frequently he invites potential community partners to visit a book club. The PC works to grow and develop the NCBC locally. The PC may expand book club activities and strategies, develop new project initiatives, and organize inter-club events. For more detailed discussion of marketing and promotion, see Chapter 13.

Program Funding

We recognize that funding can be a challenge. However, the NCBC is a relatively low-cost program that gives back enormous value to the community. The majority of the cost of running a program is paying the program coordinator, who maintains at least one book club and potentially expands the project. This part-time position may require from two to twenty hours per week. Other potential costs include books and supplies discussed above. We estimate these costs (other than administrative) to be about $200 per group, per year. Affiliates may cover these costs directly from their budget, form partnerships with outside agencies, write grant proposals, or develop specific fund-raising activities to generate funds.

Once in place, the PC assists the affiliate director or other designated affiliate staff to identify possible ongoing funding sources and participates in developing grant proposals as time allows. Local community service organizations, such as the Lions and Rotary Clubs, can be sources of funding to help cover program coordinator and training costs, purchase books, etc. Other possible sources include public libraries and literacy organizations. Some foundations have grant programs to support community efforts promoting literacy development or services for people with disabilities. Yet another option to consider is charging members a nominal fee to participate. The NCBC Central Office is available to help you develop additional funding strategies.

> *The clients love it and talk often about book club during the week. As soon as they get back they tell me what they learned. Right now they are finishing a book about Helen Keller, which they seem to really enjoy. I do have to say I was hesitant to start a book club with such lower-functioning individuals at first, but they seem to be doing just fine. The sense of belonging to a group is also a big part of it. Thanks again for taking time out to come and train us. The program is awesome!*
>
> *—Marcella T, program coordinator, Kent, Ohio*

6 Who Are NCBC Members?

Each Next Chapter Book Club has its own unique personality; therefore it's not easy to define the typical book club member. However, we are frequently asked to describe our members. To do this we've gathered information about all of the NCBC members in Franklin County, Ohio (n = 100). Group members from Franklin County are racially and ethnically diverse, with a range of literacy (and other) abilities. Some members also have physical disabilities and/or mental health diagnoses. Members range in age from fifteen to eighty-two years with about as many men as women. Next Chapter Book Club members include independent readers, those who do not read or speak, and everyone in between. Our credo is to welcome anyone with a desire to participate and make friends. Many of our members enjoy helping others in their book clubs, and all are encouraged by the achievements of fellow book club members. More than 95 percent of NCBC members are eligible for services from their local county board. (Ohio has a county-based system for providing residential, educational, employment, and social services for people with developmental disabilities. Each county is a member of the Ohio Association of County Boards of Mental Retardation and Developmental Disabilities.)

The members are all very friendly with one another. Since this group is from the day treatment program at Upreach, they have formed strong connections with each other. The members did a great job welcoming Angela to the group and making her feel welcome.

—Amy E, co-facilitator, Columbus, Ohio

They always want to know why members are missing and are always excited to see each other.

—Valerie N, co-facilitator, Gahanna, Ohio

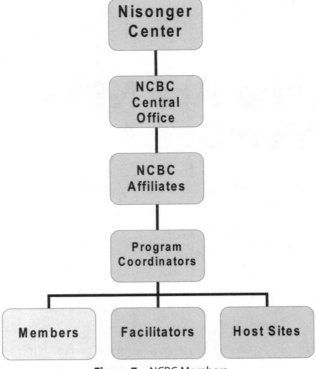

Figure 7—NCBC Members

How Do We Recruit New Members?

NCBC staff members regularly make presentations to community agencies and organizations that provide residential, vocational, and social services to people with disabilities. We have developed a strong communication network with service coordinators (case managers), who also refer potential members to us. Sometimes we post flyers and distribute brochures, but we have found that current members and word-of-mouth recommendations are the best source for new members. The recruitment process is discussed in more detail in Chapter 5.

> *All the group members know each other very well and are comfortable around each other. When Arthur started attending book club, the other members were very receptive and open to having him as a new member.*
>
> *—Amber M, co-facilitator, Gahanna, Ohio*

Profiles of NCBC Members' Literacy Levels

To help us understand and better explain the literacy skills of our members, as outlined in Chapter 1, we developed a Five-Level Scale of Literacy Skills that club facilitators can easily complete (Appendix H). In this chapter we profile members who represent each of the five literacy levels. Hopefully this will paint a picture of the range of reading abilities of our members and will help dispel any preconceived notions about who can be in a book club. Not everyone comes to the meetings for the same reasons, and not everyone gets the same thing out of them, but all members seem to enjoy themselves. The profiles are collected from a variety of sources: monthly facilitator reports, direct observations, and personal interviews.

Looking closely at the data we'd collected, we discovered that some club members have strong reading skills and leadership potential. This led us to develop a program called PALs (Peer Activity Leaders). The last part of this chapter explains the program and profiles three NCBC members who are also PAL facilitators.

Level I—No Letter Recognition or Understanding of Written Language

> *Every time another participant would ask if he wanted to read, he would say, 'No.' So finally I said, 'Roy, I will help you. I believe in you, and we can read this paragraph.' And we did. Even though the only word he knew in the entire paragraph was 'a,' the smile on his face was enough for me to know I had boosted his confidence and made him excited to read again the following week, because he knew I would be there to guide him through words he did not know, which were mostly all of the words on the pages.*
> —*Hallisy B, from her "This I Believe" audio essay, November 7, 2005, Columbus, Ohio*

Roy is a fifty-year-old man who heard about the book club from his service coordinator. School was hard for Roy as a child (he attended public school before the passage of PL 94-192, when education for people with intellectual disabilities was not mandated), and he never learned to read. But he *wanted* to learn.

Roy works in supported employment and does not need to read for his job, but reading is something he always wanted to learn. So every Friday morning (after his evening shift, before he went home) Roy came to his NCBC. The first book his club read was *Count Us In: Growing Up with Down Syndrome* by Jason Kingsley and Mitchell Levitz. Roy participated through "echo reading,"

wherein a more skilled reader read a word or phrase and Roy repeated it. He dutifully followed along the lines of text with his bookmark and always wanted to take his turn to read.

Over the course of many weeks through repeated echo reading, Roy came to recognize several recurring and short words. Roy actively participated in discussions about the book and currently sees himself as a reader. When he was asked what he would tell someone thinking about joining a book club, he responded, "Come join the club with me. Learn how to read. It's fun."

I had seven active members, with a combination of readers and nonreaders, which made the group perfect. The cutest member of the club was Justin, who could not read but would pretend to read and make up the story about the dog, Winn-Dixie. The group was so accepting of this, and would compliment Justin after he finished 'reading.' This really boosted his overall self-esteem and he was quite proud of himself.

—Linda R, program coordinator and co-facilitator, Marion County, Ohio

Level II—Recognizes and Understands Letters

Angela has been a book club member since August 2005. She is a twenty-nine-year-old adult with Down syndrome who lives with her parents and siblings. Although legally blind, Angela earned a high school diploma from a mainstream program. She is not employed, but volunteers for several organizations.

Angela's favorite places to go are the bookstore, library, and the coffee shop! She loves to be around books. The NCBC facilitators provide a successful literacy experience for Angela. Before joining the book club, Angela would go to the library every three weeks, check out six to eight books

on a topic, and pore over the pictures as her mother read to her. Now her mother reads aloud book selections from the club ahead of meetings, so Angela has an idea of what's coming. They discuss the books, and Angela tries to read them independently. Angela currently attends three book clubs each week—preparing for all of them has become a time challenge!

Angela also loves talking and joking with people. The highlight of her week is attending NCBC meetings; in fact, she wants to return from family trips early so she won't miss a meeting! Her mother Kathy has noticed that Angela is "a tad more outgoing and definitely happier, with improved social skills and a more joyful attitude." She was shy at the book club at first, but now she greets people and initiates conversations. She's more comfortable and more verbal in social settings generally. Her interactions with siblings are different, too. Angela used to be a quiet observer at family gatherings, where her family had to draw her out. Now she's more open, more of a participant. Since joining the NCBC, Angela can now read short words.

NCBC has provided opportunities for Angela to develop more self-esteem, motivation to read and think about books, encouragement to create and do art work, and have a brighter life.

—Kathy B, parent and legal guardian, Westerville, Ohio

Level III—Reads and Understands Single Words

Mark is a fifty-six-year-old man with Down syndrome who lives with his father Harley, age eighty-six. Mark grew up before public education of people with disabilities was mandated. His mother did what schooling she could with Mark at home. Mark has been a book club member for more than three years. He attends with three co-workers from the sheltered workshop where he works full-time.

Mark likes his club very much and "wouldn't want to miss it." He also really enjoys the weekly tutoring group, where he meets with people with different reading levels and personalities. Harley had been disappointed in Mark's reading progress, so enrolled him in a pilot one-on-one tutoring program at the Nisonger Center. Mark had good letter recognition and good understanding of letter sounds, but when reading aloud he would often get "stuck" on and repeat the first letter of a word.

Harley notes that Mark's reading has improved markedly, but that may be more attributable to the tutoring than the club. "The allotted time is too short to do focused tutoring," Harley says. "The club approach is good for teaching word recognition and hearing stories." During club meetings, Mark now reads more fluently and needs help with fewer words.

Before joining the book club, Mark did not read much at all. He would look at books and the comics in the newspaper and try to read Bible passages. He recently showed an interest in books about airplanes and got three from the library. He also read a sign at a store for the first time. Mark is more attentive when his father is trying to explain things, making slow but steady progress in his general behavior.

Mark enjoys and feels confident around people, but Harley thinks the NCBC helps with Mark's socialization. He says, "It's an excellent idea that it meets in a public place and away from the workshop."

> *Lucas likes the camaraderie, though he's not a social person (due to his autism). He enjoys being there, but he does not enjoy the story; he's detached from the story. Reading is a photographic activity; he understands the words, but he's not engaged.*
> —*Kathy C, support staff, Columbus, Ohio*

Level IV—Reads and Understands Sentences

Kate is a twenty-six-year-old woman with ID who has been a member of the NCBC for one year and four months. She lives in an apartment with two roommates with supported living services. Kate socialized with her brothers and a few friends from school while growing up and was enrolled in inclusive educational classes. She graduated from high school at age nineteen.

Kate learned to read as a teenager. She states that it was tough to learn but "very exciting." She joined the NCBC to try something different and for the chance to "get out to the bookstore." Kate says she reads very little outside of NCBC because she does not have many books at home and does not have the opportunity to go to the library. However, she has been reading more since she has been a member of the NCBC and would like to read even more.

Kate considers all five members of her NCBC to be friends. She says that they all become excited to finish a book together. According to Kate, her club has finished four or five books so far. Her favorite book has been *The Adventures of Tom Sawyer* and she looks forward to reading *The Adventures of Huckleberry Finn*. She also hopes to have the chance to read more about animals.

> *Joe just bought and moved into a new condo. He has been discussing the work he is doing with the book group, the staff at Caribou, and other patrons.*
> —Amy L, co-facilitator, Upper Arlington, Ohio

> *The members all LOVE to talk with each other. They share experiences, stories, and just gossip sometimes! They love to tell each other about their lives; it's great.*
> —Diana B, co-facilitator, Columbus, Ohio

Level V—Reads and Understands Paragraphs

Kurt is a forty-five-year-old man with mild ID who lives at home with his seventy-year-old mother. At age five, Kurt's teachers stated that he would never learn to read. However, Kurt did learn to read along with his older brother, and was reading aloud before he entered kindergarten. Kurt loved reading and was actively encouraged by his mother, an English teacher. He worked a paper route and played with his brothers and other children in the neighborhood while growing up. Kurt was enrolled in Special Education classes through high school and graduated at age nineteen.

Until ten years ago, Kurt worked very little outside of his home. For several years Kurt worked in a large corporate mailroom and was very satisfied with this position, which utilized his attention to detail and reading abilities. For the past two years, since being laid off from his mailroom job, Kurt has been working in an industrial enclave that does not require any reading skills and is somewhat less satisfying.

In addition to his favorite books on presidential history and mysteries, Kurt reads the newspaper every morning. He particularly enjoys the "Thought for the Day" and the sports page. He also enjoys television game shows such as "Jeopardy," and "Wheel of Fortune," which draw on his literacy skills and knowledge. Kurt states that he has been reading even more since he joined the NCBC one year ago. Kurt's favorite parts of the NCBC are talking about books and the refreshments. Despite the noise in the café, he says that it is fun to be there. Kurt's NCBC group has been reading *Little House on the Prairie*, which Kurt read and enjoyed as a young boy and has enjoyed reading again. Kurt says he enjoys "reading out loud together and talking about all the food in the book."

The NCBC serves as a social outlet for Kurt in addition to socializing with his co-workers. Kurt also participates in a weekly bowling activity, but says that he does not talk with his fellow bowlers. Kurt's mother says that he often needs to be "drawn out" in social situations. Because he has always loved to read, the NCBC offers Kurt a comfortable activity in which to socialize.

> *We have started a mother/daughter book club with five mother/teen daughter duos. This group is on their second book and prefers to meet in homes, as that is most appropriate for this age and gives the girls each the opportunity to play hostess, which they love. The girls are looking forward to 'growing up' and moving into the community sans parents in a year or two.*
>
> *—Sarajane A, program coordinator, Champaign, Illinois*

> *Laura has been involved with NCBC for a long, long time, and sometimes I am just stunned to silence by her. She has the quietest voice of us all, using a machine to project the sounds she emits, and yet she has the most focus of us all. When the coffee-grinding machines start or one of the members goes off on a tangent, even I get distracted. When I look back at her, however, there she is—trying to catch my eye so that I can pronounce a word for her. Nothing deters her.*
>
> *—Monica R, co-facilitator, Upper Arlington, Ohio*

Who Are Peer Activity Leaders (PALs)?

In 2005 we submitted a grant proposal and received funding from The Columbus Foundation for a new initiative to significantly expand and enrich the NCBC. We wanted to draw on the abilities of NCBC members to develop and implement a peer facilitator component called PALs (Peer Activity Leaders). We now recruit NCBC members to volunteer as facilitators, or PALs, and to take on leadership roles, contribute to others, and advance their own literacy, communication, and social skills. To date, we have trained a total of fourteen members in the Columbus area to serve as PALs.

Ideal candidates for this role have strong reading skills and an interest in serving their fellow NCBC members, who are encouraged by the success of their peers. The benefits of peer modeling are well established in the professional literature (Guralnick, 1990; Guralnick et al., 2006). When people with ID observe others with disabilities in a successful leadership role, it can motivate them to participate more. When peers help one another, it represents natural social support. In Hocking County, Ohio, two of the more experienced club members have started a book club at their sheltered employment workshop. (See the profile of Vera G and Kelly P in Chapter 8.) In the long term, our hope is that more NCBCs can be fully facilitated by two volunteers with ID.

This initiative required us to modify our training protocol to address issues unique to PALs and their co-facilitators. Specifically, we developed a simplified version of the existing training materials and approaches. PALs and their co-facilitators have learned to work together to maximize participant enjoyment and learning.

> We're doing really well with our new book, 'White Fang.' Everyone seems to really be enjoying it, especially the onomatopoeic words. Every time we read the word 'howl,' we all turn to Courtney and she howls at the moon like a wolf. She is our howler! That makes reading that particular word much easier and more exciting. Courtney is a lot of help with reading and getting drinks and setting up tables. I'm lucky to have a Peer Activity Leader in my group!
>
> —Leah G, co-facilitator, Columbus, Ohio

Profiles of NCBC PALs

Scott A, Columbus, Ohio

Scott A had been a Next Chapter Book Club member for about six months when he was invited to be trained as a Peer Activity Leader. He had graduated from high school in special education (EMR) and had tried a sheltered employment workshop, but it didn't work out. Instead Scott participated in a day habilitation program. He loved to read newspapers, newspapers, and more newspapers! Since joining the NCBC, he started reading books during club and would go to the library and read newspapers there. He loves reading and being with people.

Scott is excited about being a PAL. His sister Donna R says he's becoming more confident in his social relationships, he's going out more, and his behavior is becoming more socially appropriate. "He sees that he's a better reader, which helps his self-esteem and sense of self-worth." Scott lived independently in an apartment until his stroke in March 2007. After recovering in a rehab center, he now lives in an apartment with wheelchair accessibility. Though he loved being a member and co-facilitator in two book clubs, he has only been able to resume regular NCBC participation in one club.

Charles (Chuckie) D, Columbus, Ohio

Chuckie is a thirty-five-year-old man who lives at home with his parents, siblings, and several nieces and nephews. He graduated from high school in special education and took vocational training. Chuckie works full-time through a sheltered workshop as an elevator operator in a downtown office building. He also works one day a week at the NCBC office at the OSU Nisonger Center. His mother, Nora, heard about NCBC and wanted Chuckie to expand his reading and meet other people. She says, "I encourage him to be more outgoing and have more social interaction. Otherwise he's content to just stay at home and go to work." He joined in December 2005.

Before joining the book club, Chuckie would read library books in large print. It took three or four months to read them. He likes stories such as Stephen King dramas. Since he joined the book club, Nora says Chuckie picks up the newspaper and reads more independently and at a higher level: "He's reading books to his nieces and nephews; he never did that before." His interest in reading has increased dramatically. For example, he recently chose a pile of books rather than a pile of games for an activity. Nora has also noticed changes in Chuckie's general behavior: "He's more attentive and more confident. He helps more at the house with his nieces and nephews, and takes a whole lot more initiative."

His mother thinks Chuckie is more assertive since starting the book club. For example, when his sister said he couldn't do something because of his disability, he challenged her and said he could do what everyone else does. Nora says, "Chuckie's more comfortable interacting with crowds. He now interacts more at church and is not in the shadows anymore. He's willing to go out and explore more, even on the computer. He pulled up the NCBC website and showed me his picture there."

In August 2007, Chuckie helped us develop a member questionnaire. Over the next four months he did telephone interviews of sixty-three book club members. Almost everyone answered "BIG YES" to his questions about liking the book club. "It was nice to call and talk to people and get to know them," Chuckie said. "Everybody's different, and I found that interesting. One guy was telling me how he likes the book club and where he works. At the end he called me his friend, and that felt good. Basically, everybody I talked to called me a friend." (See a summary of Chuckie's results in Chapter 7 and the complete questionnaire in Appendix M.)

In October 2007, Chuckie received training to serve as a PAL for his book club. Kate B, one of the facilitators, says he's become a valued leader in the group. He says, "It's fun to be a PAL. I get to help people and learn as I go." Chuckie also represents consumers on the OSU Nisonger Center's Community Advisory Committee.

The difference in Chuckie is like day and night—he's a blossom opening up. His father and grandmother have noticed, too. Thank you for being such a positive role model in Chuckie's life.

—Nora D, parent and legal guardian, Columbus, Ohio

Kara G, Columbus, Ohio

Kara has been a book club member since October 2005 and belongs to two clubs. At age twenty, Kara is a fifth-year high school senior in a special education program. She used to volunteer at Whetstone Public Library twice a week but now works part-time with Vocational Guidance Services. Kara joined NCBC mainly for the social interaction. Her dad, Gregory, says that before joining she did not usually read on her own. Kara would sometimes read books like Harry Potter with her mother, but not on her own. "She would rather play a video game or watch TV." He says that at book club, "She gets off on being begged to read. Reading is something she's good at, so she likes to be the star."

Gregory says "Kara's usually shy in public. But in the group, she's more confident, not shy." When she was going through the job application process, she mentioned the book club activity. He says NCBC is something that might make her attractive to potential employers on a resume. "Overall she sees it as a positive experience in her life."

Kara attended training to become a PAL in October 2007. Her co-facilitators in both clubs welcomed her help. Shortly after the training, Kara decided to take responsibility for keeping attendance records. She set up a system in both clubs she co-facilitates. Her mother, Becky, says she now pays more attention to getting ready for her clubs each week. Kara says, "It's been fun to be a PAL. I've learned to respect other people." She also thinks she has improved as a reader and a leader as a result of her PAL training and experience.

How Well Has the PAL Program Worked?

Feedback from the program so far has been mostly positive. Twelve out of fourteen PALs are still co-facilitating book clubs. People emerge as PALs through their participation in the clubs and development of reading and social skills. A few of the early PALs felt uncomfortable in their new roles. We tried to select members who were not always thinking of themselves; yet getting them to be supportive of other NCBC members on a consistent basis was not easy. We've learned from this experience and adjusted our approach. We now provide a checklist during the training session to clearly explain what is expected of PALs in meetings. We offer more support, encouragement, and prompting than we originally did. PALs recruited and trained recently have made the transition more smoothly and successfully.

7 What Do NCBC Members Want To Know About Their Club?

Many people in our society believe that people with developmental disabilities are not interested in learning or books. We know that's not true. Our book club members have told us! Many adults with disabilities are living independently in the community. Yet they often lack opportunities to socialize and make friends. The Next Chapter Book Club (NCBC) can change this.

This chapter is for you, the NCBC member. For many of you, this is your first book club experience. We want you to know what you can expect and look forward to.

My favorite part of book club is reading and getting to know new people and hanging out with friends.

—Bryan, member, Columbus, Ohio

A Book Club: "What A Novel Idea"

A group of parents, professionals, students, and people with disabilities founded the NCBC with two groups in Columbus, Ohio, in 2002. Since

then, we have grown to more than one hundred thirty clubs in fifty-five cities in the United States, three cities in Canada, and four cities in Germany.

The idea is simple. A group of five to eight people gather with two volunteers. You will meet in a local bookstore, coffee shop, or café. You will read aloud and discuss a book together for one hour a week. You don't have to read anything at home, but it's great if you do. Here are the most important things you need to know:

- The Next Chapter Book Club gives you the chance to learn even after school is finished.
- Learning in the book club is a social activity in a community setting.
- The Next Chapter Book Club welcomes members with any kind of disability, or no disability.
- The Next Chapter Book Club welcomes members at any reading level, even those who need a lot of help.
- You do not have to be a good reader to enjoy the book club. People who lead the book club will help you read as much as you want.

- You are not expected to do any homework or turn anything in. Sometimes there will be outside activities you may choose to do with the group.
- You're only expected to read aloud or contribute to discussions as much as you'd like. Your participation will not be judged or graded.

I love coming to the book club so I can learn how to read. I want to read different books. I can read kids' books and adult books. I like the refreshments they have in the café.
—Rhonda, former member, Columbus, Ohio

NCBC Member Rights

As an NCBC member, you have the *right* to...

- get as much help as you want while reading and participating in the book club.
- be treated respectfully by other club members and facilitators.
- decide which book club to join, if space is available.
- decide, along with your fellow book club members, how you want your book club to run.
- decide how much and how long you want to participate.
- vote for which books you want to read.

I enjoy talking about books and about the people in the book.
—Phoebe, member, Columbus, Ohio

NCBC Member Responsibilities

As an NCBC member, you have the *responsibility* to...

- come to book club each week. If you cannot come, you should tell someone in your club.
- be respectful of your fellow book club members and facilitators and others in the bookstore or coffee shop around you.
- help make decisions about your book club.

- pay for any drinks or snacks you would like to have during book club.
- treat books with care.

I know the routine at the bookstore where my club meets, because I work there.

—Jerrrey, member, Dublin, Ohio

NCBC Member Expectations

As an NCBC member, you can *expect* to…
- learn about books and reading.
- meet new people and make friends.
- enjoy a fun activity every week.
- have fun in your community.

Because we wanted to understand what members liked about their clubs, we surveyed ninety-seven book club members from December 2004 through July 2005. Here's what they said:

- Eighty-one members (84 percent) said their reading improved as a result of being in the book club.
- Sixty-three members (65 percent) said they found new friends in the book club.
- Seventy-nine members (81 percent) said they liked or really liked meeting in the café.

The book club helps me when grocery shopping—I can start to recognize some words.

—Janice, member, Columbus, Ohio

Book Club Agreements (Sample Rules)

Clubs develop their own rules. For example, the members of one club that meets on Thursdays at 6:30 PM at Borders in Columbus, Ohio, decided on these rules:

1. Listen and follow along while others are reading.
2. Let the reader try to say the word first. Then ask if you can help.
3. Be nice, generous, and fair to each other.
4. Pay other members back if you borrow money.
5. Tell people when they read well.
6. Listen while others are speaking or telling a story.
7. Have good manners and be polite.
8. Have fun!!

I want the book club to teach me words on signs. I want to learn how to drive, and I need someone to help me read signs.

—Rob, member, Columbus, Ohio

Our Members Speak!

Charles (Chuckie) D has been a book club member since December 2005. He works part-time in the NCBC office at the OSU Nisonger Center. He also received training and serves as a Peer Activity Leader (PAL) for his book club. (You can read Chuckie's profile in Chapter 6.) In August 2007, Chuckie helped us develop a questionnaire to find out how well the program is doing and how well the members like it. He used it to interview sixty-three members in the Columbus area. You can see a copy of his questionnaire in Appendix M. Here is a summary of the results:

Chuckie's Questionnaire Results 1/25/2008 [N=63]

1. Do you like the book club? **62** "BIG YES" (98 percent); **1** "Little Yes" (2 percent)
2. Do you like your facilitator? **63** "BIG YES" (100 percent)
3. Do you like the book you're currently reading? **59** "BIG YES" (94 percent); **4** "Little Yes" (6 percent)
4. Do you like where your book club meets every week? **60** "BIG YES" (95 percent); **2** "Little Yes" (3 percent); **1** "Little No" (2 percent)

5. Are people in the bookstore friendly? **59** "BIG YES" (94 percent); **4** "Little Yes" (6 percent)

6. Do you think your reading has improved since you joined the book club? **52** "BIG YES" (83 percent); **9** "Little Yes" (14 percent); **2** "Little No" (3 percent)

7. Do you think you have more friends since you joined the book club? **62** "BIG YES" (98 percent); **1** "Little No" (2 percent)

8. Do you think you are more comfortable in public places than before you started book club? **60** "BIG YES" (95 percent); **1** "Little Yes" (2 percent); **2** "Little No" (3 percent)

9. Do you know anyone you could ask to ask to join a book club? **17** "Yes" (27 percent); **46** "No" (73 percent)

10. What would you suggest changing about your book club? **55** "Nothing" (87 percent)

11. Is there anything I can do to help you? **55** "No" (87 percent); **3** "Chuckie is a good guy" (5 percent); **1** "Be a friend" (2 percent); **1** "Help me read" (2 percent) **1** "Help me get my friend in [the club]" (2 percent)

12. Is there anything else you would like to tell me? **54** "No" (86 percent); **5** "I like it" (8 percent); **1** "He's all right" (2 percent); **1** "I am shy around people" (2 percent); **1** "It's a nice place" (2 percent)

When Bethany was recently in the hospital, everyone in the club wrote her a card. Those were the cards she kept going back to, telling us who the people were. Those were the ones she treasured—from her real group of friends.

—Eileen W, parent and legal guardian, Hilliard, Ohio

8 Who Are NCBC Facilitators?

Two or more volunteer co-facilitators lead each club. They range in age from sixteen to over eighty. In the Columbus area, 36 percent of facilitators are students, mostly in college but a few are in high school, and about 8 percent are retirees. Others are professionals, parents, siblings, homemakers, or people with disabilities. Some are employees of disability service agencies. Women constitute 72 percent and men 28 percent of facilitators. Their average length of service in a club is thirteen months, though a few have remained with the same club for several years. Facilitators do not share the same role as program coordinators, who work for the affiliate organization and are responsible for the daily operation of the NCBC program as well as local program development. (More about the role of program coordinators is discussed in Chapter 5.)

The comments and statements in this chapter are based on monthly reports that facilitators across the country submit to us on our website as well as personal interviews with facilitators conducted by telephone, in person, or by email.

Why Do We Recruit Volunteers?

We have many reasons to recruit volunteer facilitators. One is cost-effectiveness; the program can be started, maintained, and expanded in a given community with very little paid staff capital commitment. Volunteers commit to a little more than one hour per week, but their contribution is far more than the time they spend. They bring a wide range of backgrounds and experiences to the clubs and offer new ideas and fresh perspectives. For the most part they are nonprofessionals and represent the communities in which they live. Exceptions are the staff from community day programs who bring their clients to the clubs, and students in programs such as the Nisonger Center's training programs. The book club program offers a leadership-building opportunity for young professionals in the ID field. As such, it appeals to colleges and universities with service learning programs.

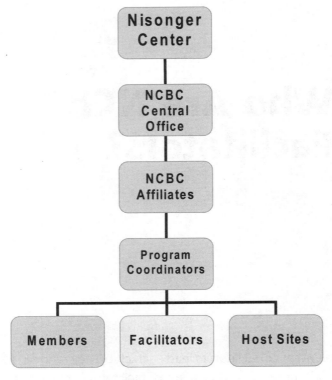

Figure 8—NCBC Facilitators

What Are the Benefits of Volunteering?

Anecdotal reports for centuries have described the beneficial effects of volunteering and contributing to the community on a person's sense of well-being and satisfaction. Now scientific findings demonstrate that "giving is good medicine." According to Stephen Post, PhD, professor of bioethics in the Case Western Reserve University School of Medicine,

> Generous behavior shines a protective light over the entire life span. The startling findings from our many studies demonstrate that if you engage in helping activities as a teen, you will still be reaping health benefits sixty or seventy years later. And no matter when you adopt a giving lifestyle, your well-being will improve, even late in life. Generous behavior is closely associated with reduced risk of illness and mortality and lower rates of depression. Even more remarkable, giving is linked to traits that undergird a successful life, such as social competence, empathy, and positive emotion. By learning to give, you become more effective at living itself (Post & Neimark, 2007).

Volunteering benefits the young, the middle-aged, and the old alike. Considerable research shows that there is a positive correlation between volunteering as a child and teenager and volunteering and donating behavior throughout one's lifetime (Fahrenthold, 2003). Researchers have argued that youth who volunteer and adults who volunteered as youth in service learning programs, for example, reap the ideological benefits of an education in moral judgment, experiential opportunities, and development of ideological motivators (Yates & Youniss, 1999, cited in Fahrenthold, 2003). A record of volunteer activities also benefits youth by helping with college and job applications (from Points of Light Foundation).

One explanation for the increased health effects among the older volunteers studied is that "volunteering is an additional social role" and provides "beneficial health effects associated with more social ties" later in life (Wilson, 2000, quoted in Graham, 2003). Grossman and Furano state that "highly organized activity [such as regular volunteering] is the single strongest predictor, other than [not] smoking, of longevity and vitality" (Grossman and Furano, 2002, quoted in Graham, 2003). Young and Glasgow (1998) report that "controlling for sociodemographic characteristics and religious participation, those who participate in instrumental community-oriented voluntary organizations have higher levels of self-reported health" (Young and Glasgow, 1998, quoted in Graham, 2003). Many studies have found that people who volunteer benefit from enhanced emotional health and life satisfaction.

> *Volunteering for the Next Chapter Book Club gave me a chance to support a literacy project that I generally would not have become involved in as a student. It also allowed me to give back to my community with something more valuable than money—time!*
> —Amber M, co-facilitator, Gahanna, Ohio

Why Do NCBC Facilitators Volunteer?

Top Ten Reasons To Facilitate an NCBC:

10. You've wanted to catch up on your reading.
 9. It's more fun than spending an hour watching reality TV.
 8. Volunteering feels good and is good for you!
 7. It only takes a little more than one hour per week.
 6. Who can't use a few more friends?
 5. Lots and lots of laughs!
 4. Groups become like families and look forward to getting together every week.
 3. It's a relaxing break from the rat race.
 2. It's a chance to be a part of a groundbreaking program.
 1. Your NCBC members will leave a lasting impression on your life.

Those are reasons we often give in facilitator training sessions. When we actually ask our facilitators, they have many motives for volunteering with the NCBC. Mary Ellen K, Amber M, and many others think the book club is a great way to give back to the community. Some, like Suzzanne F and Dean F, have a sibling with intellectual disabilities. Several facilitators are students in healthcare-related fields and want hands-on experience to complement their course work. Jillian O thought it seemed like a great way to "get her feet wet" without a lot of time commitment.

Some were already familiar with disability. For example, Erick V's aunt had Down syndrome and his mother worked as a speech therapist; Tonya A had previously volunteered with Special Olympics; Emily A had worked with children but wanted an opportunity to work with adults with disabilities;

and Becky H worked at ARC Industries and had recruited members for the club from there. David R had no previous community service and wanted to do something meaningful. Monica R wanted a chance to read for pleasure again and thought she should spend her free time helping other people rather than herself.

When asked what their motivation was for coming to book club each week, facilitators tended to answer one of these themes: "It's a lot of fun!" (Nicole B). "The members!" (Lori P). "I like to just relax and enjoy myself each week!" (Lisa J).

Why Do We Recruit Two or More Facilitators for Each Club?

We have several reasons for recruiting at least two co-facilitators per club. Our experiences have shown us that it's effective for one facilitator to focus primarily on the literacy activities during club meetings and the other on social interaction within the group. Two people can more easily hone in on members' needs and respond to them. For example, some members need more help reading, while some need more help interacting with other members or controlling their impulses. Also, having two or more trained volunteers allows facilitators to take a week off when needed. Additionally, they enjoy exchanging ideas with each other, collaborating on activities, and offering each other personal support. Here's an interview of co-facilitators, Alice L and Biru C, both high school seniors in the Columbus area, describing the social interactions in their book club:

Question: What did you do to promote social interactions between members?
ALICE: Biru and I had a variety of ideas and had little brainstorming parties. But overall we ended up just going around the table and reading out loud from the books. Every now and then we would ask the members what they thought about the pictures and how they interpreted them. Sometimes we would bring our own art supplies and have them draw what they thought about the story line.

Question: What about social interactions that don't have to do with reading?
BIRU: One of the best things we did was after we finished the first book, which was *The Wind in the Willows*, we had a little party at Alice's house. We had food, we watched the movie of the book, and that was really, really, really fun. I think they loved it, and it was...
ALICE: ...a celebration to acknowledge that they finished the book and a great accomplishment.

Question: What strategy was most successful to promote actual friendships among members?
BIRU: I think the name tag making was useful in helping them learn each other's names, which always feels nice to be welcomed to the group. Also, every week we would ask what's going on and they'd talk about it and that's how they'd know more about each other. And, when we got to a part of the book where we discussed a meal, for example, we'd stop and say, "So Pete, what's your favorite food?" And he'd say, "Pizza," and someone else would say, "I like

pizza, too." So we'd start conversations off topics from the book, and that would always lead to interesting topics.

As I mentioned earlier, this club was more than just reading books. Every week people would come in and be really excited to talk about something new that happened in their lives. People genuinely seemed to really care about what was going on with everyone else. One week, a lady named Crystal told us that she got engaged and that she was so excited about her wedding. Week after week we would ask her how things were progressing and she would show us her ring. It was really endearing to hear all these little stories of what's happening in their lives.

Question: Can you think of any other specific stories like that, where there was a lot of social interaction?

ALICE: Definitely. In *The Wind in the Willows*, you have many interesting and colorful characters, and I remember one part where Mr. Toad is driving a car. People would say, "Oh, I like cars, too!" And others would say, "Oh, this is what I like." Then we would go around and just kind of share our favorite pastimes, and branch off into what we were doing this past weekend. Then people would introduce the other people in their lives and tell us stories about them. So, there were many times when we went off on a tangent and just had a little chat instead of focusing on the book.

Question: And did you feel that it was OK not to just focus on reading?

ALICE: Oh, definitely, I think that's what makes it. Instead of just reading you have other social interaction...

BIRU: . . . a friendship group as well. We are there as facilitators and to lead, but the best times are when we get to sit back and not do any talking and they talk among themselves. For example, in the very beginning, we basically said, "Let's read *The Wind in the Willows*," and they were all very open to that idea. But after we read that book we said, "So what do you want to read next?" By this time they were so comfortable with each other that they each had different ideas. We had five or six different suggestions of what to read. We had the best time! We got to just sit back and they talked among themselves as to why their chosen book was better. It was nice to see them each take action, take the lead more, and talk about what they wanted to do.

How Does This Experience Compare with What Facilitators Expect?

In preparation for their NCBC service, volunteers have the opportunity to observe one or more clubs and receive about ninety minutes of training with the program coordinator. Despite this common training, each facilitator's experience may differ from their expectations. Some facilitators with a background in health care or social work say it's about what they expected. Several, like Monica R, were apprehensive at first about their abilities to lead a group of adults with

developmental disabilities. Suzzanne F had trepidations because, while she had a lot of experience with her sister, she had never lived with or spent time with somebody else with a disability. Rachel K was rather nervous at first and unsure of the participants' abilities to read and talk about books. Jillian O did not expect to have to discuss behavior problems with one of the members. Katrina B didn't expect such a broad range of individuals participating, "We have everything from autism and highly skilled people to those who are severely retarded." Bill C was somewhat disappointed that the members of his group were more interested in the social aspect than in reading or learning to read. Amber M assumed that it would take time for her to adjust to being with people with ID; however, she found them "quite easy to work with and a lot of fun!"

Many former and current facilitators claim to get a lot more out of it than they expected. Several mention overcoming the stereotype that the people would be more developmentally disabled. "They put me in my place! We all enjoy the same things, so don't be so quick to judge others." (T'Nita W)

How Does This Experience Relate to Other Aspects of Facilitators' Lives?

The experience was very rewarding and I plan to continue the club on a volunteer basis when I retire.
—Linda R, program coordinator and co-facilitator, Marion County, Ohio

The NCBC enriches the lives of student facilitators. Tonya A, for example, thinks that "Exposure to people with disabilities in a social context rather than a therapeutic one is a good component that I think is missing from the graduate program." Rachel K says, "The NCBC provided enjoyment with the population with disabilities—it wasn't like work." Monica R said,

The book club humbles every self-serving thing I do. I know graduating and finding a job are my top priorities, but they are not my only priorities. The ability to cultivate relationships with people who rely on me enriches my life exponentially. No matter how busy I am, I know I have a group of people sitting at a table each week expecting me to be there. I can't tell you how much that helps me put things into perspective.

The student facilitators report that they expect their NCBC experience will help them with their careers, whether in health care, social work, or special education. David R says, "In hospital administration, it's easy to lose sight of what you're doing. The book club highlights what's really important." Becky H says, "The NCBC gives me experience in other aspects of people's lives outside of work, and there've been positive surprises. For example, conflicts with each other at work don't carry over—they're very supportive of each other in the group." Cortney C now works with a vocational rehabilitation group helping people with disabilities to live independently. She says, "I learned how to work with adults with disabilities, so it was directly relevant." Tonya A works in a hospital as a rehabilitation counselor for employees with an injury, illness, or disability. Sometimes her patients come with their mother or another family member who is involved in their care. She says, "It reminds me that some book club participants arrived with support staff, and that sometimes these people need to be included in the conversation." Mark F says, "Because we met in a public space, it helped me understand public perception and how to develop a program like this. As a program director, I now work in a facility that is 25 percent residential and 75 percent community-based." Katrina B thinks the NCBC helps in her current role as a hospital administrator, not to jump to conclusions too quickly and to be more informed about this important population. T'Nita agrees; she learned not to judge people based on appearance or superficial factors. "When things don't go well, you need to have a 'Plan B.' This helps with my administrative training and my job in Phoenix." After graduation, Monica R moved to Poland to teach English as a second language. She says,

> The experience I had with NCBC really helped prepare me for the spontaneity of the classroom more than I could have ever imagined. Teaching and being with people for the sake of learning qualifies as a continual training course in human understanding. I love it almost as much as sitting at a coffee table reading *Moby Dick* with the Caribou Coffee clubbers.

> *NCBC has had a HUGE impact on me and has made me rethink my major here at OSU. I recently switched my major from Music Ed to Special Ed with a minor in music. I'm currently looking for a job and ... I was thinking yesterday walking back from class about possibly being a service provider.*
> —Grace U, co-facilitator, Columbus, Ohio

The NCBC also enriches the lives of nonstudent facilitators. Mary Ellen K is a parent of typically developing children who had no previous experience working with people with disabilities. She used her NCBC volunteer experience as one of the qualifications that enabled her to secure a full-time job with Franklin County Educational Services Center in Columbus, Ohio, as a teachers' assistant (para-professional) in special education. Mary Ellen says,

> Our club is awesome. Every week I look forward to hearing about everyone's activities. The time we spend together is always full of laughter and fun. My friends from our club are some of the most sincere and caring people I have had an opportunity to meet. Thank you for helping to enrich my life with the joy of helping others to discover the joy of reading.

> *It seems no matter what kind of day I'm having, I leave book club in a better mood every time!*
> —Alisha B, co-facilitator, Columbus, Ohio

What Would Current Facilitators Say to Prospective Ones?

Facilitator responses to this question were overwhelmingly positive. Some common themes include, "Wonderful experience, great for everyone" (David R). "You'll feel good about yourself" (Cortney C). "Extremely enjoyable and rewarding—maybe even addictive!" (Vicki G). "Don't be afraid; people with disabilities are just like anyone else" (Rachel K). "Make sure you are committed to it; if you lack consistency, the program won't be as effective. Don't worry about offending anyone and messing up" (Katrina B). "You'd be surprised how one hour per week can drastically change the way you think about people with disabilities and their right to be included in all aspects of society" (Jillian O). "Great emotional return for very little investment" (Bill C). "You will meet some wonderful people who will make you laugh and open your eyes about what is really important in life" (Melissa F). Tonya A says,

> GO FOR IT! It's an experience like nothing else. If you have no interaction with people with disabilities, you may have doubts about what to say. The level of acceptance is amazing and a learning process for everyone. Everyone will have different experiences, but they will all be positive!

Profiles of NCBC Facilitators

Suzzanne R, Mike F, and Mikey F, Columbus, Ohio

Suzzanne R has a twin sister with mental retardation. She never intended to go into the field, but ended up working in the Ohio Department of Mental Retardation for more than twelve years. In the summer of 2003, she attended a presentation and picked up a Next Chapter Book Club brochure.

She found the "little blurb" intriguing and called, then visited a few clubs and took the facilitator training. Suzzanne was engaged to marry Mike F, who has a son named Mikey. Among other reasons to volunteer with the book club, she wanted to see how Mike and Mikey would do with somebody like her sister who will eventually live with them.

When we interviewed all three in July 2004, Suzzanne said, "The book club is just sort of a natural extension of us now. We've actually been doing it almost a year, and it's just been a great time for us to get together. And we're friends with everybody so it's nice."

Mike got involved in the book club because of Suzzanne, but he had no idea whether he'd be able to help or have the skills to help. He learned that it takes "just a little patience and an interest and commitment." Mike said, "The biggest thing for me is I've been able to learn of the remarkable abilities that reside in people whom I think a lot of people in society tend to write off. And if you take your time with a lot of these folks, reading and talking to them, they know a lot more and they have a lot more to contribute than I think anybody is remotely aware of."

Mikey, age fourteen, said, "My dad dragged me into this at first, and I didn't think it was going to be that much fun. But it turned out to be lots of fun, because everybody there has their own personality. The group just keeps growing, and we've just become better friends as the books go on."

Suzzanne emphasized that they didn't want the experience for members to be, "We sit with our book, and we're very rigid, and we read." She said it's more like social time: "We get together and we hang out, we have Monday night together. And it's really interesting to see how everybody can absorb different experiences."

Suzzanne and Mike invited the entire club to their wedding and even incorporated the wedding into club activities. Suzzanne explained, "We usually try to get into the groove until the whole group has arrived; we do a little writing time. We all have little note cards and we write out words." Mikey continued, "Some of our words have themes, like this last week we did a wedding theme. And we had words like *bride, bridesmaid, groom, wedding*, etc."

On the fourth of July they had a party at their house and read the Declaration of Independence together. Suzzanne said, "That was wild! We went through each of the elements, like why we were mad at England and what we were saying we weren't going to stand for anymore, and we talked about 'atrocities' and some of the really big words." Mike added, "And they talked about tyranny . . . you know, what does that mean? And they kind of got it, either through context or whatever, which is good—that's what you want them to do."

When asked how much their members enjoy the club on a scale of one to ten, Mike immediately replied, "Eleven!" When we probed to find out what differentiates *this* activity from going to a movie or just getting together once a week, he said, "In a certain way, I think they feel empowered, because they feel like this is, in essence, taking charge of their lives. They're learning something, they're doing something, and they're going someplace they want to go. And when they're there, I think they feel fairly free to express themselves, and that makes them feel empowered." Mike continued, "I think that's the key: They feel respected by us and certainly by the other members of the group."

> *Our time together is a strong reminder of the incredible diversity and talent within people, just waiting for an opportunity to be realized. We have all become real friends and, to a great extent, have positively changed each other's lives.*
> —*Suzzanne, Mike, and Mikey F, co-facilitators, Columbus, Ohio*

Emily A, Columbus, Ohio

Emily A was a graduate student in Health Services Administration at The Ohio State University and a trainee in LEND, the Nisonger Center's graduate interdisciplinary pediatric training program. She had the opportunity to take over facilitating an existing group during the school year and recruited Erich V as her co-facilitator. She and Erich then recruited classmate David R as a summer sub-

stitute; he liked it so much that he stayed on in the fall. They later recruited T'Nita W, also from the Health Services Administration department.

Emily had worked with children with disabilities before and wanted the opportunity to work with adults. She had expected the book club to be more like babysitting—keeping people on task, giving guidance and direction; instead it was more mutual, sharing stories and friendship. She says, "It's personally rewarding to be helping people and learning about an underrepresented population. I had no exposure or interaction as a child, so this was a wake-up call. It applies directly to my career in policy and long-term care; it's important to understand their issues and difficulties." After graduation, Emily took a job as a healthcare administrator in Memphis and is in the process of bringing the Next Chapter Book Club to her community.

Bill C, Columbus, Ohio

Bill C is a retiree who read about the NCBC in an article in the *Columbus Dispatch* and found it intriguing. He had had some experience tutoring a person with "mental handicaps" one-on-one in Massachusetts. Bill says participating in this activity changed his ideas about literacy. He used to think that people could either read or not. Now he's learned it's more complicated: Some people can read mechanically but have no understanding of the words or comprehension of the story. He found it most helpful to try to help the members get "into the story" more—to use their imaginations and place themselves inside the atmosphere of the book.

Volunteering has given Bill a high level of satisfaction in doing something helpful in the community. And he's learned a great deal about the world of people with intellectual disabilities.

Dean F, Blacklick, Ohio

Dean F's brother, Jeffrey, was in assisted living since age fourteen in Port Clinton, Ohio. Their parents died, then Jeff's roommate died, his case worker retired, and his care provider left town, so Jeff moved to Franklin County. Jeff had no peer relationships in Franklin County after moving there. Friendship Connection groups were "cliquey." He joined the NCBC mainly for social interaction; reading was a bonus.

Jeff had always been sweet and social, so he made new friends easily. He asks about people who aren't at the club and wants Dean to call to ask if they're alright. Before joining the club, he would

read *People Magazine* and coupons in the Sunday newspaper. When asked how Jeff's reading had changed since beginning the book club, Dean said, "I have been astounded at the dramatic impact it's had. The difference between when he started reading aloud compared to now, is remarkable."

Dean never intended to get involved—he just took Jeff to meetings and sat on the sidelines. Then, one of the facilitators left. He said, "I was impressed with it and enjoyed it, so I became a volunteer facilitator. Now I have new friends, too. It's the greatest thing I've ever been involved in."

> *Each group has their own 'flavor' or 'personality.' The facilitators for the third group are our most unique. One is a fifty-ish-year-old guy who is a paraplegic and the other is a home-schooled high school girl who has severe dyslexia and didn't read until she was about eleven. She is now on fire about reading and can't wait to work with the group. These two will be, I believe, the perfect facilitators for the group. They each have something in common with the participants and they bonded very well during the training.*
> *—Nann M, program coordinator and co-facilitator, Monroe, Louisiana*

Vera G and Kelly P, Logan (Hocking County), Ohio

Vera G and Kelly P are active members of an adult book club that meets regularly at the Great Expectations Book Store, Café and More in Logan, Ohio. They are also retired teachers and customers of the store. One day, the activities director of the Hocking County Board of MR/DD approached the owner of the store about hosting a Next Chapter Book Club. Jillian Ober, the trainer from the NCBC Central Office, came to Logan to conduct the training session. Vera said, "Jillian's enthusiasm was contagious. When we met the clients, we were hooked." Since Hocking County is largely rural, the members were transported from their sheltered employment workshop site by van to the bookstore on Friday mornings. Kelly said, "We had known many of the participants (originally six young women) through our teaching experiences. This was an opportunity to interact with them in a social setting. Their reading skills increased immensely. We agree that the experience exceeded our expectations."

The book club became so popular that they outgrew the bookstore and are now meeting at a downtown café. And others in the community are getting involved. The Hocking County chapter

of Delta Kappa Gamma donated $300 to purchase books and book bags for their local NCBC group. Journals were donated as well. (At the conclusion of each meeting, each member gets to choose a sticker to be added to his journal.) Other retired teachers have donated sets of books and stickers. This has been a tremendous incentive for Vera and Kelly, who later applied for and received another $300 grant from the Ohio State membership of Delta Kappa Gamma." The book club members were invited to a dinner meeting of the Hocking County chapter of Delta Kappa Gamma, where they shared about their experiences with the book club. The attendees were all responsive and everyone enjoyed the reports."

At some point, NCBC stopped being volunteer service to me and instead became something that I just do to brighten the week ... kind of like yoga!

—*Monica R, co-facilitator, Upper Arlington, Ohio*

9 What Do NCBC Facilitators Do?

Volunteer facilitators play a key role in the implementation of a Next Chapter Book Club. In fact, the program would be impossible without you! The first thing we ask prospective volunteers to do is visit one of the active clubs in the area to get a feel for what a club is like and to decide if it's right for you. After the observation, we schedule a sixty- to ninety-minute training session with the local program coordinator. The training is individualized based on your experience leading a group and experience with people with disabilities. We also ask that volunteers agree to a background check, such as ink-free fingerprinting. (Other sources of background checks are acceptable.)

This chapter, directed to facilitators, summarizes and supplements the training and orientation provided by the program coordinator. It describes the steps involved in leading a group, explains the roles of a co-facilitator, and provides guidelines and suggestions for creating an enjoyable book club experience for members. The enthusiasm and commitment, however, must come from you—the volunteer. We encourage you to seek support from the NCBC program coordinator throughout the volunteer experience.

Step 1: Examine Your Motivation for Becoming an NCBC Facilitator

Facilitating an NCBC is a rewarding yet sometimes challenging experience. It's important to understand that you are committing to facilitate the book club *until the book is finished*, which takes approximately twelve to fourteen weeks. Members will get to know you and look forward to coming to book club each week. We encourage you to carefully consider your decision and ask yourself the following questions:

- Why do I want to become an NCBC facilitator?
- What qualities do I hope to bring to the book club members?

- What am I hoping to learn or gain from this experience?
- Have I made a plan to include the NCBC in my schedule each week?
- Do I have any fears or worries about becoming an NCBC facilitator?

Other questions may arise once you visit a book club and observe NCBC facilitators and members in action. Please feel free to ask questions or share any concerns you may have with your NCBC program coordinator.

Step 2: Prepare Yourself and Your Club

To be well prepared to facilitate your NCBC group, we ask that you do the following:

Attend a Training Session with the Program Coordinator

During this sixty- to ninety-minute training session, the program coordinator discusses guidelines and strategies for facilitating your group; addresses topics such as confidentiality, facilitator and member rights and responsibilities; and answers questions and addresses any concerns you may have. (More about the role of program coordinators can be found in Chapter 5.)

At this time, or soon after, you should meet your co-facilitator, and we encourage you to use this time to get to know one another and prepare for your group. You will be assigned a host site for your group; however, you and your co-facilitator and the program coordinator will decide on a time that is convenient for you and the members, unless you are joining an existing club with an established meeting time. We recommend that you avoid the busiest times of day for your host site, if possible. While it's important to take into account prospective members' schedules, it will not always be possible to satisfy everyone.

> *The training was well-structured with many examples of how different clubs operate and what to expect as a facilitator. I think it prepared me very well and I would not change the format.*
> —Melissa F, co-facilitator, Columbus, Ohio

Next Chapter Book Club
Facilitator Intake Form

1. Name:
2. Phone number:
3. Address:
4. Email:
5. Occupation:
6. How would you describe yourself?
7. Have you been involved with individuals with MR/DD i
   If yes, how?
8. What experience have you had with volunteer work?
9. How did you hear about the NCBC?
10. What concerns, if any, do you have about facilitating a
11. When would you like to begin facilitating a book club?
12. What days and/or evenings and times are you availabl

Appendix C (p. 166)

Complete a Facilitator Intake Form (Appendix C)

This form provides the program coordinator with information regarding your availability, background, interests, experience with people with disabilities, and training needs. The form may also assist the program coordinator in matching co-facilitators.

Conduct a Self-Evaluation

After you have attended the training session, ask yourself the following questions to determine your readiness:

- What unanswered questions do I have?
- What challenges might I face?

■ How will I deal with these challenges if they arise?

You may wish to speak with your program coordinator about any remaining questions or reservations. However, keep in mind that you'll learn most of what you need to know "on the job," and many of your questions will be answered at your first book club meeting.

> *The training was informative, but I think it takes just jumping in and doing it to really learn what it's all about.*
>
> —*Nicole B, co-facilitator, Columbus, Ohio*

Introduce Yourself

Before your first meeting, call each member to introduce yourself and let them know where and when you will be meeting. The program coordinator will let you know if you need to speak with family or support staff at this time to be sure they are aware of the member's weekly commitment. At your first meeting, share a little bit about your hobbies or favorite movies, for example, and ask your members to do the same.

Allow Members To Decide How the Group Will Run

NCBC members have multiple opportunities to engage in self-determination and self-advocacy. Ask members how they would like to read the book. Typically, groups enjoy reading the books aloud, as this encourages maximum participation and mutual support.

At your first meeting, explain to members that they can participate to whatever degree they feel comfortable. The reading levels of members will vary, and it's important to let everyone know that help is available to all who want it. You may involve "emergent" readers by asking them questions about the pictures, having them repeat words or phrases after they are read, or asking them to pass out the books. You'll find more strategies and activities for emergent readers (readers who require support) in Chapter 12.

> *The book club is good for Karen, because she is capable of learning but unable to express her knowledge. We don't know what she understands and gets out of it. Her previous staff said she didn't read while at book club. I suggested she get her drink or snack AFTER she reads, and she started reading aloud that week!*
>
> —*Marilyn T, support staff, Columbus, Ohio*

Group norms, such as where members sit and the way they begin each meeting, will develop as members feel more at ease with each other and with you as a facilitator. These norms are a sign of comfort and connection.

Although we want members to have control over their book club, we suggest that you set a few guidelines, write them down, and review them from time to time as needed. One club's list of rules is in Chapter 7; here are some suggested guidelines:

■ Only one person talks at a time.

■ We do not make fun of anyone's reading ability.

■ There are no bad or stupid questions.

Step 3: Facilitate Your Group

Whether you are new to leading a group or you already possess some experience, it's likely that you'll learn many things about yourself and the group process while facilitating your book club. Throughout this process, it's important to have a calm and positive attitude, as your members will follow your lead. Although we suggest guidelines in this chapter, we recognize that each group will be different. We encourage you to allow the members of your club to create the kind of group that works best for them.

Support Your Book Club Members

The primary role of the facilitator is to support members and encourage literacy learning, social connectedness, and community inclusion for the length of at least one book. The following are recommended strategies for doing just that.

Literacy and Communication Strategies

Many NCBC members express a desire to improve their literacy skills. The challenge to facilitators and the group at large is to incorporate literacy skills and learning into the social community atmosphere of a group meeting. Facilitators have used the strategies in this section to encourage literacy and communication skills among members as a natural extension of NCBC meetings. They are designed to encourage participation, interaction, and learning in natural contexts—not isolated, skill-based teaching. (For detailed descriptions and expanded activities, see Chapter 12.)

> *I always made a point of encouraging members by thanking them and telling them how wonderful their reading was. I did see that increased confidence helped make members more comfortable about reading out loud.*
>
> —*Charu A, co-facilitator, Gahanna, Ohio*

Communicatively Match Group Members.

- *Facilitators should try to communicate with members using similar vocabulary levels and length of sentences.* This helps to assure that you are communicating effectively and that you understand each other. When facilitators use some of the same words members use and keep sentence length about the same as the members, it increases the likelihood that the members can respond to the facilitator's comments.
- *Talk about the story to show members what kinds of things to say.*
- *"Match-up" by adding one or two more comments to the conversation.* Facilitators want to add comments based on the communication level of the member. Matching up suggests adding new or unfamiliar content to a comment but doing so using sentences and vocabulary familiar to the member. It can also mean using slightly different vocabulary or sentence structure to reinforce an idea.
- *Use new words in context.* It's easier for members to learn new words when they know the subject context. For example: When discussing a story, explain a new word using what is known or has just been discussed about the story.

- *Extend a topic by making one more comment.* One way for members to learn to have longer conversations is to learn to say one more sentence or comment beyond what they typically would say on a particular topic.

Respond to All Verbal and Nonverbal Communication.

- *Give members words for their experiences.* When a member is having difficulty expressing himself, try putting into words what you think he means. If you are correct he will agree and perhaps elaborate. If you are incorrect he will try again to communicate what he intended.
- *Treat events in the book as bridges to personal stories.* Encourage members to discuss how the story relates to their lives. For example, "Have you ever been in a tornado like Dorothy?" or "Wilbur really needs Charlotte's help. Who do you go to when you need help?" This is a great way for members and facilitators to get to know each other.
- *Teach words (oral and written) that are immediately useful.* Seize the moment when a member is struggling to express himself by providing a useful word for the member to use. Teaching five new vocabulary words by rote is less helpful than teaching one word in context as the need arises.
- *Translate members' nonverbal communication into words.* If a member looks puzzled, stop and say, "Jose, do you understand what we are discussing?" Often when a member cannot say what he wants, we can read his facial expressions or body language and try to put that into words for him.
- *Return the member to the topic when he strays.*
- *Except, do not respond to inappropriate or undesired talk.* (More on this in Chapter 16.)

Make Communication Balanced and Reciprocal.

- *Say something, and then wait for a member to respond.* Giving members a little extra time to respond significantly increases their talking. Deciding how long to wait is tricky. We want to "hold the member's place" while he is thinking, but we don't want to lose the attention of the group. The facilitator has to get a "feel" for how much time to wait for a member and still keep the group's attention.
- *Talk in a turn-taking exchange with members to model conversation skills.*
- *Limit members from talking in monologues.* You'll need to set explicit ground rules for how long each member can talk without others participating. For example: "Give us two sentences about your weekend." (More on this in Chapter 16.)
- *Keep everyone involved in the discussion.* This may require redirecting comments to individuals, cuing members to wait patiently for another member to talk, interpreting and connecting content for members to encourage their participation. (See Chapter 16.)

Engage Members Emotionally.

- *Be animated in your conversations.*
- *Encourage members to share their feelings.*
- *Point out emotional content in the stories.*

General

- *Start with the strategies to encourage literacy and communication skills that come most naturally for you.*
- *Watch how members respond, and keep using strategies that work.*
- *Try new strategies and activities when little is happening,* such as the ones we describe in detail in Chapter 12. There are many ways to be effective at supporting literacy and social interaction.

- *Be patient and show that you feel energized by every new skill your club members demonstrate.*
- *Avoid making your club members feel that you're testing their skills.* Generally this means stop asking questions and instead comment on members' comments. Members may have mixed feelings about the time they spent in school; at NCBC we want to create natural learning opportunities and avoid question-and-answer type scenarios.
- *Praise all members equally.* Don't overly encourage skilled readers and inadvertently point out or ignore others' deficits.
- *Although members' literacy skills may improve, focus on* reading to learn, *not learning to read.*
- *Remember that the ultimate goal is not accuracy; it is for members to interact more frequently and in new ways with books and stories, each other, and the community around them.*

The other day Del read the word 'condition' without any help and was so excited when he realized it was correct that he laughed and gave me a hug. What a great guy!
                                                    —Melissa F, co-facilitator, Columbus, Ohio

Social Connectedness Strategies

The Next Chapter Book Club gives members opportunities to meet new people, build friendships, engage in a popular pastime, and gain a sense of belonging. We encourage our members to interact with each other during and outside of the club. You may want to facilitate conversations between members who have similar interests. Though you may want to begin your meetings with social exchange, you should also encourage members to talk about the book. Ask questions and encourage members to share their thoughts and feelings about events and characters from the book. We encourage you to keep the mood casual and seize opportunities for laughter.

Recognize and reward participation whenever feasible. For many members, participation may feel risky. Your positive responses are an excellent way to encourage efforts to become a part of the group. As your group becomes more familiar with the process, you may want to ask members to take more responsibility for running the group. Members may also serve informally as "facilitators" and ask volunteers to read or help them read aloud. (In some cases we have trained members to serve as Peer Activity Leaders, or PALs. Read more about PALs in Chapter 6.) They may also take turns calling each other each week to remind everyone about book club. The more of the process that group members facilitate, the better!

Your program coordinator may provide bookmarks or note cards for you to distribute to your group members. On the reverse side, ask members to write their names and phone numbers. (You may need to assist some members.) These bookmarks can serve as a roster of who is in the book club and allow members to contact each other outside of group if they choose. In Columbus, the program coordinator provides each facilitator with an updated roster anytime the group's membership changes; facilitators can then make copies of the roster for their members.

The lists below summarize several strategies to encourage social connectedness. (For detailed descriptions and more activities, see Chapter 12.)

Encourage Members To Observe One Another and Model Appropriate Behavior.
- *Support members in helping each other sound out words and follow along with the text.*
- *Model conversational skills and reinforce members when they ask questions and converse with each other.* A powerful reinforcer is allowing conversations to develop and continue for a short while. Anytime we pay attention and participate in an interaction, we reinforce it.
- *Encourage members to help each other navigate through the bookstore or café.*
- *Encourage members to order and purchase their own refreshments.*

Encourage Participation.
- *Use gentle encouragers, such as, "Jane, would you like to try this sentence with me?"*
- *Make comments to open up the conversation; ask open-ended or "either/or" questions.* For example: "Geri, tell us about your weekend with your sister." Or, "Pam, do you like coffee or hot chocolate better?"
- *Reward participation* through attention, allowing a member to read first, or verbal praise.

Promote Friendships.
- *Exchange phone numbers and encourage members to call each other.*
- *Initiate conversations by pointing out mutual interests.*
- *Make sure members know each other's names.* You could use name tags or one of the strategies outlined in Chapter 12 to help members learn and remember each other's names.

Community Inclusion Strategies
Natural and inviting community settings are central to the NCBC model. Next Chapter Book Club host sites include bookstores, cafés, and coffee shops such as Borders, Barnes & Noble, Panera Bread, Target Café, Caribou Coffee, Starbucks, and other locally owned small businesses. We do *not* meet in isolated settings such as workshops, service agencies, individual homes, libraries, schools, churches, etc. (A few exceptions are explained in Chapter 10.)

Benefits to members include a meaningful engagement in the community and opportunities to practice social skills. Meeting in the community also strengthens the social aspects of the literacy experience. Benefits to communities include increased exposure to and awareness of people with disabilities, opportunities for attitude change, and enhanced diversity within the community. (For detailed descriptions of strategies and activities for community inclusion, see Chapter 12.)

Basic Group Process Guidelines

The NCBC offers members many opportunities for choice and decision-making. Although our volunteer facilitators are group leaders, it is really up to the members to decide how their meetings will go. As a facilitator, you will help your members decide

- which book they want to read. (See "Book Selection" later in this chapter and the "*Choose the Next Book*" activity, item 49 in Chapter 12.)
- how they read the book. (Examples: "Do we go around the table, or do we raise our hands and volunteer to read?" "Do we want to review the words we learned last week?")
- how they want to organize meetings. (Examples: "How much time do we want to spend socializing?" "Do we want to do that at the beginning or at the end?")
- how much they want to read, talk, and share. (Some members are more comfortable with these activities than others.)

Troubleshooting Behavioral Issues

It's important to stay flexible and remember that your group may run differently each week. Members may become disruptive or lose focus from time to time. If a member becomes disruptive, attempt to redirect him by asking if he would like to read, or ask a specific question about how the book might reflect aspects of his own life. Try to draw him back into the group discussion. Though it is rare, if a member cannot be redirected, you may need to locate the member's family or support staff for suggestions. Sometimes family and support staff browse through the bookstore or sit and have a coffee while the member is in the club. In this case, you can talk to the family or support staff at the end (or start) of a meeting to gain insights regarding how to redirect the member's disruptive behavior. If the family or staff member does not stay nearby during the club meeting, you can ask to talk with him when he brings the member the next week or could call him. Also, contact your NCBC program coordinator between club meetings to discuss the situation and determine appropriate behavioral support strategies.

If a member becomes bored or loses focus, it may be helpful to engage him in a conversation to spark his interest again. Keep things fun by throwing in an activity from time to time. Facilitators may have a drawing to win a prize, organize a game or discussion, or bring a special snack. (See Chapter 12 for more activity ideas.)

Although conflict can be distressing to facilitators, it's a typical component of any group. Look for teaching and learning opportunities; most conflict you will encounter can be used as a tool to expand discussion. When kept in the proper context and within group rules, conflict can be valuable by allowing group members to learn from each other's unique perspectives and experiences. However, if the conflict exceeds the level of usefulness for discussion or has become a personal issue for one or more members, do not hesitate to redirect members or change the topic entirely.

As a facilitator, your most important task is to encourage members to learn and have fun by creating a safe and comfortable environment! (More advice about these types of situations is discussed briefly in Chapter 16.)

I cannot express in words what it means as a parent to have my daughter, Jennifer, be part of this group. Because of her disabilities, Jennifer has had a hard time finding social, recreational opportunities to participate in with her peers. Jennifer has dual diagnoses with some mental health issues. She had been in denial or not accepting of people with multiple disabilities. But she has been accepting of everyone in her book club.
—Peggy M, parent and legal guardian, Columbus, Ohio

Manage Your Book Club

For the continued success of the NCBC, it's important that you monitor your group's progress and member participation. In addition to the support you provide your members during book club, we ask facilitators to do the following tasks:

Monitoring Attendance and Group Membership

Because this is a voluntary activity, NCBC groups are "open." Members are free to leave the book club if they choose. It's a good idea to keep a weekly record of attendance. If you notice any extended absences, we suggest that you contact the member, or ask the program coordinator to do so. We want to find out why that person is no longer participating in book club, and hopefully address any concerns or scheduling conflicts he may have.

Any time a member leaves the group, it's important to let remaining members know, so they are not left wondering what has happened to their fellow member. When a new person joins the group, be sure to ask the new member to introduce himself. Prompt existing members to introduce themselves and discuss what has been going on in the book. If *you* decide to leave the book club, be sure to give members at least two to three weeks advance notice. The bonds you form with your members may be very strong, and you will want to give all parties enough time to process your departure from the group.

Weekly Phone Reminders

Call all group members weekly the day before your group meets to remind members (and their support staff or guardian if appropriate) of the book club. This promotes attendance and may become an appropriate activity for one or more of your group members to take over once the group is better established. Occasionally one of the facilitators may need to call the member who is supposed to call all of the group members to remind him that he needs to call, review the script of what he will say, and reinforce the rule regarding appropriate calling times that the group established.

Monthly Facilitator Reports

Once a month, facilitators submit Monthly Facilitator Reports (Appendix E). These reports are essential for the monitoring and development of the book clubs. You can complete them online in the Resources section of our website, www.nextchapterbookclub.org, photocopy and fill out the form from Appendix E at the back of this book, or print a copy from the included CD-ROM. Facilitators give these forms to their program coordinator (PC), who then shares this information with the program director (or affiliate organization director) and the Advisory Board to continuously improve the program's effectiveness.

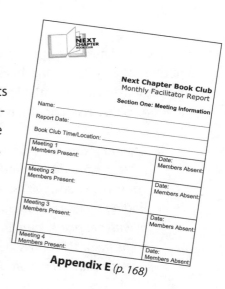

Appendix E *(p. 168)*

Book Selection

Notify NCBC staff when your group is close to finishing a book. The program coordinator will send you a list of currently available titles for your group to choose from. Discuss these book options with members and decide on the top three choices for the next book to be read. Members will typically vote on which book they want to read next, and the book with the most votes wins. (For details, see the "*Choose the Next Book*" activity, item 49 in Chapter 12.)

Appendix F *(p. 171)*

End-of-Book Surveys and Certificates of Completion (Optional)

These surveys provide needed information for the NCBC program coordinator to evaluate the success of the program. Typically facilitators read the surveys to members and record their answers during a meeting. Please see Appendix F for a copy of the survey. Although each club decides how to observe the finishing of a book, often we do so with a small celebration and award a certificate at the host site. Appendix G has a template you may use to create certificates of completion. Many clubs enjoy renting or borrowing from the library a copy of the movie version of the book for their celebrations.

Appendix G *(p. 172)*

Janie's proud to finish a book and likes the certificates and parties to celebrate.

—*Marianne T, sister and legal guardian,*
Columbus, Ohio

Develop a Working Relationship with Your Co-Facilitator

A supportive partnership between co-facilitators is essential for the success of a book club. It's important that you feel comfortable with each other and that you get to know your co-facilitator during or after the training session. If you feel you have been matched inappropriately, please allow a week or two to see if the situation improves. If not, be sure to express your concerns to the program coordinator and request reassignment.

Support One Another

Book clubs run more smoothly when co-facilitators support each other and share the responsibilities of the club. This means assisting each other during challenging situations and moments of uncertainty. Co-facilitators also support one another by sharing their creativity and encouraging a fun atmosphere. Between meetings we encourage facilitators to discuss how the meetings went and to develop a plan for the following week. They can refer to the training manual, chat with other facilitators on the website, or contact the PC if specific questions arise.

Negotiate Roles and Responsibility for Group Tasks

Co-facilitators should decide how to divide the weekly group management responsibilities, such as calling members each week to encourage attendance and completing the monthly evaluation forms. (See Appendix E for Monthly Facilitator Report.) Co-facilitators should also consider taking turns with different roles during the weekly meetings. For example, one person can be the *Primary Literacy Facilitator* and focus on reading, de-coding, writing, and other literacy-related behaviors. The other can be the *Primary Social Facilitator* and focus on conversations, helping behaviors (such as locating start and stop points in the book or referencing a word or letter being profiled for a member), and friendship-building behaviors among members. These tasks may be spontaneous or you may prepare activities in advance.

Communicate with Next Chapter Book Club Staff

We ask facilitators to complete a Monthly Facilitator Report to help us monitor weekly participation and attendance. These reports also provide a forum to document changes in member skills and behavior, and to ask for help when needed. As part of program monitoring and evaluation, we ask facilitators to respond to periodic inquiries from NCBC staff to share successes or to complete member and facilitator satisfaction surveys. NCBC staff members also try to visit each local club regularly.

Step 4: Become Involved in Recruiting New NCBC Members and Facilitators

Your support and enthusiasm are important for the growth and development of new book clubs. You can participate in the recruiting of new members in the following ways:

- Ask the members of your group to bring someone new to the club.
- Follow up with individuals who have expressed interest in joining, or refer them to the program coordinator.

- Hand out NCBC flyers and encourage members to tell their co-workers and friends about it.
- Make sure group members are having fun; if the members are enjoying themselves, they will tell others.

You can participate in recruiting new facilitators by

- talking about your experience to friends, co-workers, and family members. Word of mouth is often our most effective recruiting tool.
- asking interested persons to visit your group. Chances are they will become motivated to get involved by what they see at your group!

So here I was, the founder of this pretty cool program, and I had yet to facilitate my own club. Sure, I had filled in for volunteer facilitators, had observed numerous clubs, and demonstrated how to facilitate an NCBC in conjunction with a few trainings. Yet I had not experienced the week-to-week inner-workings of a club. That is, not until May 22, 2006. Yes, the 22nd of May was my 'coming out' party, and I was actually pretty excited.

The reason for my jumping in and getting my feet wet was the fact that two facilitators who had been running one of our clubs in Columbus, Ohio, needed to leave around the same time. So, I was thinking this should be easy and fun. Little did I know that initially the experience was anything but easy and fun. I found myself nervous and at times at a loss for what to say or do. It was as if I was frozen in time. I thought things would come naturally. Then it dawned on me that I had never been formally trained as an NCBC facilitator! It took me several weeks to get in sync with my club. There is no doubt the training would have helped by alerting me to the uncertainty I might feel and by giving me the facilitation tools I needed.

—Tom Fish, program director and co-facilitator, Columbus, Ohio

Above all, as an NCBC facilitator, you should be yourself and allow your members to be themselves. The beauty of the NCBC is that each club has a mood and a culture of its own.

10 What Are NCBC Host Sites?

One group has a benefactor, whom the group calls 'Grandpa Bob.' He is at Joe Muggs the same time they are every week and has bought the coffee or other drinks for the group. He also checks in and wants to make sure that everyone is doing well. At first he was hoping to 'fix' the group, but then he realized the members weren't broken, they just did things differently.
—Nann M, program coordinator and co-facilitator, Monroe, Louisiana

A host site is a bookstore, coffee shop, or café where an NCBC meets. Many clubs meet at national or regional chains like Barnes & Noble, Borders, Caribou Coffee, Panera Bread, Starbucks, Target, and local coffee shops or bookstores. We also have clubs that meet in cafés within libraries.

What Does a Host Site Do?

The term "host site" might be somewhat misleading, because the sites do not actually greet our members at the door or show them to their seats. Arrangements with our local host sites are very informal, with no binding agreements. We do not ask anything, and in return, they do not ask anything from us. However, the outcomes for both parties are hugely beneficial and reciprocal. Some host sites have more than one weekly NCBC meeting at their bookstore, café, or coffee shop.

What Are the Benefits to Host Sites?

Being a host site for NCBC helps a business build a customer base with a diverse population of members who come every week, make purchases, and enjoy positive interactions with employees and other customers. Families and support staff of book club members also purchase

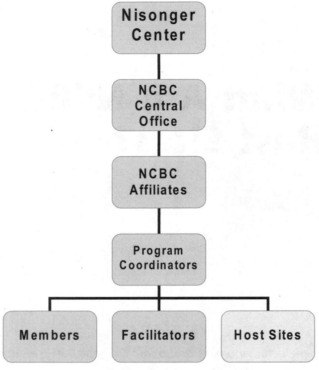

Figure 9—NCBC Host Sites

drinks, food, and books regularly. In addition, host sites help promote public awareness of people with disabilities among their customers and employees. Customers often recognize and appreciate this act of community support.

> *I believe they are very comfortable in the setting, and we are generally very visibly seated in the middle of the café. Most of the members' parents or caregivers at least go with the members to order, because they pay for the beverages. But some of the members do order their own drinks.*
>
> —Lisa J, co-facilitator, Columbus, Ohio

How Do Host Sites Respond to the NCBC?

Whether at a bookstore, café, or coffee shop, we are always conscious of the fact that we are both guests and customers. We do not expect to be treated any differently than any other group of people who may be meeting at a local establishment. We try to not be overly boisterous or loud, but we do not ask our members to whisper while they are reading and talking with one another.

> *I've never noticed a negative reaction but often notice people smiling encouragingly when they see the group. Most people don't notice, though; they are focused on what they are at Target for.*
>
> —Susan M, co-facilitator, Columbus, Ohio

The first two Next Chapter Book Clubs in Columbus met in a Borders Books and Music café.

With one exception, we have met with no resistance from the bookstores and cafés where NCBCs are held. Our philosophy is that we have a right to be in these public spaces as much as any other group. However, we realize that it is important not to put our clubs in situations where they might feel unwanted or unaccepted. For this reason, we are neither confrontational nor apologetic about our presence in the various host sites we use. The program coordinator should be positive and upbeat when approaching a store manager. We do this as both an introduction and a courtesy to explain our program and share that we plan to meet regularly at their facility. We want the manager to be clear about who we are and what we will be doing. More about this process is discussed in the section below, "How Should I Approach a Host Site Manager?"

Often, members and facilitators become friendly with the host sites employees who make and sell the coffee. As a result of these relationships, it's not unusual for those employees to reserve tables prior to our arrival. They are our friends and we are their friends. And a few host site employees have even shown an interest in facilitating a book club.

> *All the members get along well with the host site staff, and the staff is very understanding of members' needs. In one instance, a member bought the wrong flavor soda and the staff was very helpful in making sure he got the right one in exchange.*
> *—Amber M, co-facilitator, Gahanna, Ohio*

In one of the Target stores where we meet, the café attendant happens to be the parent of a child with autism. She frequently provides our club with free food and beverages. In a Barnes & Noble café, the customer service manager pays for a small coffee or other beverage for each member and facilitator each week, without being asked. This is not something we asked for, but things like this happen.

Once, a male club member in a wheelchair had a toileting accident during the meeting. Both facilitators were female. A male café employee offered to take the member to the bathroom and help him clean up. There was no fuss or fanfare; it was just people helping people.

Why Not Meet in Libraries and Community Centers?

An administrator from a large city library system visited us to learn more about the NCBC. Our self-advocate and long-time book club member, Steve Cooley, was at the meeting. When the librarian seemed puzzled about why we usually do not hold club meetings in libraries, without saying a word, Steve put his index finger in front of his mouth to indicate silence.

That gesture symbolizes why NCBCs meet in bookstores and cafés. The book clubs are not about being quiet or closed off in an isolated meeting room. We want to see and be seen, to experience community life like everyone else. This is one of the very reasons we don't meet in private homes either. We want to buy a cup of coffee, make a wisecrack, and talk openly with one another. When someone in a club gets too loud, we tell them "not so loud." But we never whisper and we never apologize for reading aloud or discussing books (or anything else).

However, we do have a few successful clubs across the country that meet in libraries. Many libraries now have gathering areas where customers may talk freely, and some libraries have cafés and coffee shops as well. In those cases a library location works well for a book club.

The staff has all been wonderful to our group. They are nice and patient with us. Most customers are also very accommodating. Sometimes our discussions, and especially our laughter, get loud and although people are studying or reading, no one has ever been upset with us.

—Melissa F, co-facilitator, Columbus, Ohio

What Are the Disadvantages of Bookstores and Cafés?

Clearly, there are drawbacks to meeting in bookstores and cafés. We are not assured of having a meeting spot every week. (Usually we pull three or four tables together.) We try to avoid sitting in a corner, as corners represent seclusion. Although we don't ask for such favors, in some host site settings, employees put "Reserved" signs on tables prior to our club's arrival.

Another drawback to meeting in bookstores and cafés is the noise factor. Espresso machines can be loud, and this may make it difficult for members to hear each other while reading aloud. Also, there can be a lot of activity, which may be distracting for some members.

One day while we were standing in line to order food, Ashley giggled quite a bit and cracked jokes. A customer behind us smiled while watching her. When it was Ashley's turn to order her drink, she didn't have enough money. The customer behind us saw the monetary conundrum and gave her the two dollars she needed! I thought it was quite a sweet gesture on her part and nice to see people show such generosity.
—Amber M, co-facilitator, Gahanna, Ohio

A group of people reading a book out loud together in the middle of a café *does* tend to attract attention! We get our share of stares, and sometimes people who are studying and sipping coffee get a look on their faces as if they are thinking, "What the heck are these people doing, and why don't they keep quiet?" We really have never encountered a scene or direct complaint, so we put up with the occasional stare or look of annoyance.

I don't mind them reading out loud at all. It's a great place to come and read.
—Jerry M, Lake Shore Coffee House customer, Michigan City, Indiana
(quoted in Colleen Mair, "Reading it up," The Herald Argus. 29 June 2007.)

What About Meeting in Restaurants?

From the outset, it was never our intention to emphasize food and beverages with the book club. At the same time, we recognized the importance of having a beverage in the context of a social get-together. We try to avoid meeting in restaurants with sit-down service. The rationale is that the focus of NCBC should not be primarily about eating, as this can distract from reading and socializing. Other considerations with restaurants are competition for tables during peak mealtimes and wait staff not getting their usual turnover. The only circumstance under which we would be comfortable with a club meeting in a restaurant is if that is the only suitable public setting available in the community.

The Marion Diner has been so accommodating to our group and fallen in love with the participants and looks forward to our club utilizing the restaurant on a weekly basis.
—Linda R, program coordinator and co-facilitator, Marion County, Ohio

When we first started the NCBC, we bought beverages for members, thinking that would be an incentive for them to attend. We used grant money for this purpose, not realizing how much it would eventually cost. What happened was that members were ordering fancy coffee or smoothie drinks costing three or four dollars each! As we were forced to stop buying drinks, members found ways to buy their own. This taught us a valuable lesson: Do not assume a benevolent approach with people with ID. Put them in a position where they have to be resourceful, responsible for remembering to bring money, and able to determine what they can afford.

> *One facilitator wrote to Panera Bread and asked if they might donate coffee to the club members. They declined but printed bookmarks saying, 'Panera Bread proudly sponsors the Next Chapter Book Club,' showing four cups of coffee and a fifth marked 'FREE.' The clear message was, like everyone else, if you buy four cups, the fifth cup is free.*

Are There Exceptions to the NCBC Host Site Rule?

While we strongly prefer that NCBCs meet in public, community gathering places, we have considered exceptions on a case-by-case basis. One club in Columbus, for example, consists of workshop employees who all use wheelchairs. We grant them permission to meet in their workshop, because their van cannot take all four wheelchairs to a café at the same time. Another club meets in a coffee shop every other week and in a student lounge at the Ohio State School for the Blind on alternate weeks. This is because the students who are blind require additional staff support, and the school's staff and transportation resources are limited.

In spite of our insistent message about where the NCBCs should meet, we continue to have people suggesting we meet in more segregated settings. For those who insist on meeting in less inclusive environments, we request that they do not refer to their club as a Next Chapter Book Club.

Profiles of NCBC Host Sites

Defiance, Ohio

Our first club outside of Columbus, Ohio, was started in Defiance, a small town in northwestern Ohio. Ms. Chris Palmer, MSW, is a social worker for the local county board of MR/DD. She had a working relationship with Tom Fish over many years on issues related to brothers and sisters with dis-

abilities. When Tom described his book club to her, Chris immediately decided this was a program she wanted to bring to her small town of about 16,000. Because Chris taught part-time at Defiance College, she saw the benefit of involving students as book club facilitators. She originally wanted to start a club in the new coffee shop at the college library; how-

ever, the library coffee shop was not yet available when Chris recruited the volunteer facilitators and members. Chris arranged the initial training in a classroom building at Defiance College.

Chris and her colleagues decided that they would meet at the local Big Boy Family Restaurant. While we usually discourage meeting in a restaurant, the Big Boy was the only reasonable location in town. Initially, a number of members failed to leave adequate tips for the server, in addition to taking up considerable table space in the restaurant for extended periods. Each week, the server became increasingly perturbed with the situation (although Chris had spoken with the manager beforehand). When Chris found out about this, she explained the purpose of NCBC to the server and told the club members that they were responsible for tipping the server weekly. (Chris also made up for previous tips lost.) Once informed and compensated, the server became the club's new best friend and looked forward to seeing them every week. When the club did finally leave (because the college library opened), the server at Big Boy was actually sad to see them go.

Logan, Ohio

In another small town, Logan, Ohio, it took more than a year to get the book club started. Ms. Vicki Grosh, the county MR/DD superintendent and long-time friend of Tom Fish, wanted to start an NCBC at a local bookstore café. Vicki and Tom went together to talk with the owner of a quaint bookstore located in an old Victorian home. The owner was receptive to the idea and looked forward to having the club meet in the small café on the first floor. Unfortunately, by the time Vicki was able to

recruit two former local schoolteachers to facilitate the club and arrange transportation for the members, the bookstore owner decided to move to another location. Several months passed before the bookstore moved out to a new flea market just outside of town. Finally, the Logan NCBC got started and has been going strong ever since. In fact, the two facilitators, one of the members, and Vicki gave a talk at the state MR/DD conference about their experiences with the NCBC and what it has meant to them personally and to their community. (Read the profile of Logan's co-facilitators, Vera G and Kelly P, in Chapter 8.)

Monroe, Louisiana

Aliscia Banks, Executive Director of Families Helping Families of Northeast LA, Inc., first learned about NCBC in a newsletter. She and Nann McMullen, a group facilitator and Adult Opportunity Coordinator at Families Helping Families, decided to hold their book club meetings at the Joe Muggs café inside Books-A-Million for a simple reason: "At that time," Nann says, "Books-A-Million was the only coffee shop in town!" Though there are now several Starbucks in town, the convenience of parking and book selection have kept them coming back to Books-A-Million. Nann continues,

> Things have been awesome there for the most part; the employees have really
> come to embrace us. Rarely do the coffee shop employees grind coffee while we
> are reading. They realize that the noise makes it hard for the group to hear. One
> employee, who has been rude on occasion (but he is rude to everyone, not just us),
> had a seizure right as we were
> getting there for book club. Of
> course, the store called 911, and
> there was quite a bit of drama.
> When he returned to work (fine),
> each of the members sought
> him out to make sure that he
> was OK and told him that they
> missed him and they knew
> what seizures were like. He now
> speaks to us and is almost nice!
> I know it's not much, but it is a
> step forward for him.

Nann says it seems that as each new person is trained, the outgoing employee lets them know about the book club. 'Grandpa Bob,' the benefactor, now buys the coffee for both groups that meet at Books-A-Million and regularly brings treats. Nann relates "another incident that was really cool":

> A local attorney had run for judge, and it seemed that his strategy meetings were always at Books-A-Million during the Tuesday group time. We got to know him and he got to know us. One day, one of the ladies in our group went up to the counter and waited her turn to tell the staff person that our tables were sticky and needed to be wiped. The staff person turned his back and ignored her. The next person in line was this attorney, and the employee asked how he could help him. The attorney said that he would place his order as soon as the employee fulfilled the request that the young lady had made—which the employee promptly did.

How Do I Select a Host Site?

Usually the program coordinator contacts a local bookstore, coffee shop, or café and arranges to meet with the manager or owner. We recommend considering the following before selecting a host site:

- Is it open during hours that you want to meet?
- Does it have adequate space to accommodate ten people?
- Will space be available at the site during the time you are considering? (Some locations and times are busier than others.)
- Is the meeting space centrally located, rather than off in a corner or behind doors?
- Does the space seem warm, receptive, and inviting?
- Are chairs and tables moveable, so you can assemble four or five tables for everyone in the group to sit together?
- Is there anything about the location that the members might find intimidating, such as long lines to buy drinks or excessively loud?
- Are the building and bathrooms easily accessible?
- Is the site wheelchair accessible?
- Is the site conveniently located for the members and volunteers?
- Is the site close to public transportation?
- Is the space clean and neat?
- Do customers appear comfortable to congregate and linger at the site?
- Would adolescents and adults with disabilities feel welcome there?

How Should I Approach a Host Site Manager?

The host site staff here described Thursdays as their favorite day of the week because of book club!

—*Leah G, co-facilitator, Columbus, Ohio*

Here are steps to consider when talking with a host site manager or store owner:

1. Call ahead to determine a good time to meet with the manager. You may choose to make an appointment, but we generally find that such formality is unnecessary and may heighten anxiety for the manager as well as you.

2. Bring your business card and information about your agency or organization. Use this opportunity to explain what your agency or organization does and who you serve.

3. Bring an NCBC brochure. Because your contact with the host site may take place before your affiliate receives training, you can download more information from the NCBC website, www.nextchapterbookclub.org, to leave with the manager.

4. Rehearse what you are going to say, but remember that the store manager or owner may have limited time. Here is an example of what you might say:

> Hi! I am (name) and I am with (organization). We are putting together a book club for about five to eight people with intellectual disabilities. We are hoping to have the book club meet here in your store/café for one hour every week (mention the day and time if known). The club will be facilitated by two volunteers from the community and will be supervised by me or someone in my agency. The group will be reading out loud and the members will be buying drinks and maybe snacks. The purpose of the book club is to give folks a chance to read or learn to read, socialize with friends, and meet in a community setting like your store. The name of the group is the Next Chapter Book Club, and there are already a lot of established clubs across the community. I have brought some literature about the program, and you can check out the website as well at www.nextchapterbookclub.org.
>
> I would be happy to answer any questions you might have, but assure you that this will be an extremely meaningful experience for our members and volunteers. We do not anticipate any inconvenience for your employees or other customers. NCBCs across the country are held at such places as Barnes & Noble, Target, Starbucks, Borders, and Panera Bread as well as locally owned bookstores and cafés.
>
> What do you think? I think you will be quite pleased to host an NCBC, because it will expand your customer base and add to the overall diversity of your clientele. It is a meaningful experience and a win-win proposition for everyone. As we move forward, I encourage you to contact me with any questions or concerns about the Next Chapter Book Club you might have.

Profile of an NCBC Host Site Manager

Tony C, Caribou Coffee, Upper Arlington, Ohio

Tony, night manager at Caribou Coffee, first heard about the Next Chapter Book Club when meetings started there more than three years ago. He says he tries to accommodate the group. For example, because they have no large table, the staff assembles several small tables before the club

arrives. Tony says he appreciates the opportunity to see everybody socialize and participate like other people. "We usually have a good time," he says. "One girl gives me hard time about making her coffee latte improperly—there's a lot of teasing."

When asked what he would tell someone who is thinking about hosting a Next Chapter Book Club, Tony says he "would tell them to do it—especially in summer when business is slow. The book club folks are cleaner than high school kids, who leave the place trashed!"

> *The site staff is always very friendly. I don't really notice the customer response. There are always a lot of people at Caribou, and it can be very loud. People don't seem aware that we are trying to hear people reading.*
>
> *—Amy L, co-facilitator, Upper Arlington, Ohio*

11 What Is the Role of Families and Support Staff?

I love NCBC and think it's wonderful. It's affirming to have people with disabilities given the opportunity to read and enjoy getting together in coffee shops. This is an evolutionary breakthrough; really cutting-edge. Socialization is harder than when Laura was in school; this is a great opportunity to bring adults together.

—Jan D, parent and legal guardian, Columbus, Ohio

NCBC relies heavily on the families and support staff of our members. They help us in many ways. First, parents and support staff are our members' primary source of transportation to and from club meetings. If they don't bring our members, then we don't have book clubs; it's as simple as that. In some ways, the commitment by families and support staff to the NCBC is as important as that of our facilitators and members. To foster this commitment, we try to provide regular feedback about how members are doing to families and staff as well as to solicit input from them.

Second, input and feedback from families and support staff both guide and reinforce what we do. We are continually amazed by the most consistent thing they report: how much members look forward to the NCBC.

"Laura does not want to miss book club; it's a commitment. It's her independent choice to maintain that commitment—'her thing'" (Jan D). "Jessie loves it; I'm sorry I didn't do it earlier. I jumped at the chance when the Gahanna group started" (Minda B). "I think it's enriched his life" ('Shannon' K).

The main thing with Scott is his feeling good about going to something he considers to be an educational experience. Even though he can't read well, he likes to be a part of a reading group. He will take books with him places even though he can't read them. He likes to feel more educated.
—Cecil T, parent, Columbus, Ohio

Families and support staff also repeatedly acknowledge the impact of NCBC on the member's reading ability. "Before joining the book club, Jerry never attempted to read anything. Now he can read mail and see what is for him and what is for his neighbor" ('Bernie' B). "Ashley has improved in reading. She's determined to learn to read" (Carol P). "Before joining the book club, Aisha didn't read. She graduated from high school, but they just passed her through. She reads better now, at a higher level, but I'm not sure how much she understands what she reads" (Marsha H).

With the consent of members, we encourage facilitators to engage families and support staff to ask about how members are doing, and to be open and responsive to their ideas and suggestions. At times we may need to discuss concerns about members regarding issues such as behavior and attendance. When this happens, facilitators and/or coordinating staff can discuss these matters openly because of the respect and dialogue that has been established with the families and support staff.

Sarah's taking a break for two and a half months during Special Olympics for the basketball team. She's met new people in the book club and has a sense of feeling needed. She wants to be sure she'll still be needed to help when she goes back. [Sarah had PAL training and was a co-facilitator with Tom Fish for several weeks. She has come back to her club since this interview.]
—Sally G, parent, Westerville, Ohio

Third, families and support staff are our most effective marketing tool. They help our program grow by telling others about NCBC and are more credible than any brochure could ever be. This is true at the local level as well as statewide and nationally. Parents share their stories, likes and dislikes, and new programming with one another at conferences, through newsletters, and over the web. Nothing promotes a product better than satisfied customers!

I've observed an increased willingness on Kim's part to read and attempt to read things she didn't before. She has mentioned more than once that she has read out loud (with support from the fantastic volunteers) at Next Chapter Book Club. She asks for help to read recipes and doesn't want or need as much help as she did before. When we are in the car she reads the vanity plates with better accuracy. She is in charge of retrieving the mail at home. When she calls me at work she often is able to give me a pretty good idea about who has sent letters and packages. Please share our thanks with all your very important volunteer and meeting site sponsors. It has made such a positive difference in Kimberly's (and my) life.

—Lynn C, parent and legal guardian, Columbus, Ohio

Finally, families and support staff can be instrumental in assuring that the experience of being in the NCBC will generalize to other activities in a person's life. While the NCBC meets only once a week for one hour, it should not be the only literacy, community, or friendship experience that a member has. Families and support staff can help ensure that it isn't by incorporating specific activities and skill-building exercises into a member's Individual Service Plan (ISP) that promote literacy, friendship development, and community participation. Examples include regular trips to the library, meeting friends at coffee shops, calling fellow NCBC members, reading together, writing letters, exchanging birthday cards, and participating in a phone tree. (See the *"Start a Phone Tree"* activity, item 38 in Chapter 12.) They can also promote responsibility and a sense of belonging by reminding the NCBC member to call ahead to let someone know if he is unable to attend a session. In addition, families and support staff can encourage the generalization process by pointing out how and when literacy, friendship development, and community participation relate to other activities in a member's life, such as school, work, church, shopping, etc.

Arthur is also working at the YMCA and socializing with people in Special Olympics and master swimming. His social life feels easier and more accepting all around.

—Elaine D, parent and legal guardian, Blacklick, Ohio

To keep families and support staff involved and feeling appreciated, facilitators can engage them in regular conversation about the experience. Consider asking questions, such as the following:

- How does Steve like the NCBC?
- What changes have you noticed since Shelly started NCBC?
- Does Sal look forward to coming?
- Does he share what they read and talked about in his club?
- How is it working out getting Sean here every week?
- What do you think about the NCBC?
- What questions do you have about NCBC?
- What would you change or make different about NCBC?

As a facilitator, be sure families and support staff feel free to share feedback with you or the program coordinator anytime they like. And encourage them to let you know if they can think of other members or potential facilitators for your or other clubs.

I'm excited that Gillian has a place to go and meet with people. This is something she can do for the rest of her life. She had enough confidence recently that she performed the lead in 'Annie' in the community theater.

—Kathryn K, parent and legal guardian, Dublin, Ohio

It often amazes me that the NCBC works, because reading is often a really difficult pursuit for this population; they get so much out of something like this. I never would have predicted that this would work. My friend in Cleveland's daughter gave up horseback riding class on a conflicting night, because she didn't want to miss the book club, even though she reads less than my daughter does.

—Donna W, parent and legal guardian, Dublin, Ohio

12 What Strategies and Activities Do Book Clubs Use?

Strategies and Activities That Encourage Reading

We have learned much about how to teach children to read, but we know much less about effective strategies for teaching adults. A recent search on how to teach children to read by the National Reading Panel (NRP), using a defined screening process, yielded more than 400 studies for review. In comparison, a search by the Reading Research working group yielded only seventy studies on adult reading instruction and assessment that met the criteria for quality research—even when the research criteria were expanded to include descriptive studies of reading instruction.

Research indicates that the learning processes for emergent readers (both children and adults) are similar. Adults and children who are learning to read generally demonstrate poor phonics knowledge, although the adults may have a more extensive knowledge of sight words. To become a fluent reader, capable of decoding and comprehending print, several literacy skills are necessary: awareness of phonemes (the sounds that letters and letter combinations make), word analysis, knowledge of the alphabet, vocabulary, and comprehension skills. Although these skills may take time to develop, all can be taught and learned (Kruidenier, 2002).

Many NCBC members express a desire to improve their literacy skills. The challenge to facilitators and the group at large is to incorporate literacy skills and learning into the social community atmosphere of a group meeting. To meet this need, the NCBC Central Office developed a variety of strategies and activities that encourage reading. We also asked our facilitators to share with us activities that they have found useful and fun in their groups. These literacy learning activities and strategies support the NCBC model, as they encourage the attitude of lifelong, capable learners who are interested in interacting with others and participating in their communities. We organized them into activities for readers and activities for emergent readers. For members who are readers, we organized activities further into those for comprehension, vocabulary, and phonemic awareness.

Facilitators have used the activities in this section in various ways to encourage literacy skills among members as a natural extension of NCBC meetings. They are designed to encourage participation, interaction, and learning in natural contexts—not isolated, skill-based teaching. Most facilitators spend a few minutes incorporating a strategy into the typical reading routine of the club. This might actually occur two or three times in a meeting. However, there are days when we might spend the majority of a meeting creating a birthday card or writing in a notebook. Some groups have a distinct "learning how to read" focus, while others may stop to discuss or socialize more. Some facilitators ask members to purchase a blank notebook to use for various skill-building activities and bring it to each club meeting. Others purchase index cards or a small dry erase board for use during meetings, and some facilitators use both index cards and notebook activities.

Because we meet in public places, we encourage facilitators to use materials that "fit" with the meeting place. For example, paper (or index cards) and pens do not draw undue attention when meeting at Barnes & Noble, but carrying in a dry erase board might. Part of our goal is to facilitate members' fitting into a community setting, so we are sensitive to how our activities and props encourage members' blending into their environment.

As a facilitator, you'll learn to "read" your group and implement activities and strategies based on the skill level of members and your particular group process. We encourage you to tuck this book into your NCBC bag when you head out the door for book club; this way you'll have all these wonderful techniques and ideas at the ready.

For Members Who Are Readers: Activities To Increase Comprehension

I like understanding the book.   —*Van B, member, Columbus, Ohio*

1. Facilitator Reading
- ➤ **Description:** The facilitators read (and model) fluent reading of a few sentences or a paragraph.
- ➤ **Expected outcome:** Listening to reading provides the members with the opportunity to learn and ask questions about the story. Members also potentially learn new vocabulary and develop oral language skills.
- ➤ **Materials needed:** The book being read and attentive members.
- ➤ **Time required:** Depending on how long the facilitator reads and the discussion that follows, this can take from a few minutes to ten minutes.

'There's no doubt that reading aloud teaches. And there's no doubt that little kids—and big ones—love being read aloud to.' (Fox, M. Reading Magic. 2001)

2. Who, What, When, Where, How
- ➤ **Description:** After a member reads, the facilitator asks specific "who, what, when, where, how" questions to the group. Emergent readers can respond to these questions as well as readers.

➤ **Expected outcome:** Learning to answer these questions helps members understand the story (and possible alternative outcomes). The discussion around the book or story is fertile ground for learning.

➤ **Materials needed:** The book being read and a facilitator who knows the story.

➤ **Time required:** One to five minutes, depending on the discussion.

3. Relate Reading to Personal Stories

➤ **Description:** After reading a portion of a book, a member tells a personal story that relates to what was read.

➤ **Expected outcome:** Being able to extend what one reads to one's own life and circumstances creates rich learning experiences and may inspire discussion among group members.

➤ **Materials needed:** The book being read and a willingness to share some aspects of personal experience.

➤ **Time required:** From a few minutes to several, depending on the experiences raised for discussion.

4. To Your Left

➤ **Description:** The facilitator turns to her left and asks the member to tell the group about a character about whom the group has been reading. Members take turns adding information about the character until everyone has had a turn.

➤ **Expected outcome:** Members learn to pay attention to the story and to listen to each other.

➤ **Materials needed:** The book being read and members listening and responding 'on topic' to each other.

➤ **Time required:** Five to ten minutes, depending on the size of the club and how much members talk.

5. History Lesson: Yesterday and Today

➤ **Description:** The facilitator chooses some interesting subject, for example transportation, and asks the group to compare kinds of transportation described in the story (such as the covered wagon in *Little House on the Prairie*) to methods of transportation used by members of the club.

➤ **Expected outcome:** Members learn to discuss a topic from the story and relate it to their own life.

➤ **Materials needed:** The book being read and member participation.

➤ **Time required:** From a few minutes to ten minutes, depending on the level of interest of the group.

6. Round Table

➤ **Description:** Go around the table and ask each member to read just one sentence.

➤ **Expected outcome:** This technique picks up the pace, keeps everyone involved, and ensures that each member has an opportunity to read.

➤ **Materials needed:** The book being read.

➤ **Time required:** Five to ten minutes.

7. Poetry

➤ **Description:** Facilitate a poetry workshop. Poem topics may relate to the book being read, but often members become creative and write about other topics. Members can dictate to the facilitator or another member or write the poem themselves. The poems may or may not rhyme.

➤ **Expected outcome:** Creative expression; discussion of the poem within the group.

➤ **Materials needed:** Paper and pens or pencils.

➤ **Time required:** Thirty minutes to one hour.

8. Punctuation

➤ **Description:** Put a period, comma, colon, semi-colon, quotation mark, question mark, and exclamation mark on index cards or bookmarks. Make them large and colorful, as some members have trouble seeing the small marks in their books. At a point in the story where punctuation is used, hold up the appropriate card and pause to explain what the punctuation means in context. The facilitator can vocally model the meaning of the punctuation using pitch, pause, change in tone of voice, etc.

➤ **Expected outcome:** Members learn how authors use punctuation to give a story some of its meaning.

➤ **Materials needed:** Book being read, index cards, pencils, and pens.

➤ **Time required:** Five to ten minutes.

'Word sorts' help beginning readers to focus on the word and every letter in it. It's amazing how it's helping Jessie, Jeff, and Ashley. And Jessie, our 'lowest' reader, always amazes me the most when she gets things right! All of these literacy activities really pay off in the end when they read a little better.

—Amy L, co-facilitator, Gahanna, Ohio

For Members Who Are Readers: Activities To Increase Vocabulary

9. Word of the Week

➤ **Description:** The facilitator or a member chooses a word from the book being read (ideally a word that reappears in the story) and the group defines the word.

➤ **Expected outcome:** Members learn a new vocabulary word that will reappear in the story, so its meaning can be reinforced.

➤ **Materials needed:** The book being read and member participation.

➤ **Time required:** Two to three minutes.

10. Build a Word List

➤ **Description:** One group member keeps a list of new or unfamiliar words and their meanings from the story. When someone identifies a new, unknown word in the story, one member copies it on a piece of paper. Another member uses the dictionary to look up the meaning of the word and reports this back to the group. Members can also practice using the word in a sentence. One member keeps the folder and brings it to each club meeting.

➤ **Expected outcome:** Members learn new vocabulary and how to use organizational strategies for learning.

➤ **Materials needed:** The story being read, paper, pens or pencils, a notebook or folder to bring to each book club, and a dictionary.

➤ **Time required:** Depending on how the practice activities are structured, this activity can take a few minutes to ten minutes.

11. Spell or Write Words

➤ **Description:** Each member chooses a word she would like to write. It could be the name of her favorite character or one she chooses randomly by putting her finger down on the page. It could be a word she doesn't know or a word she thinks looks funny. Every member writes the word in a spiral notebook. Members can repeat the letters and instruct each other in the proper spelling (and writing) of the word.

➤ **Expected outcome:** Members learn how to spell and write words and might then recognize them in print. Members also learn letters and the sounds that letters make, and they learn how to write letters and words.

➤ **Materials needed:** The story being read, notebooks, and a variety of pens and pencils.

➤ **Time required:** Five to ten minutes, depending on how many words members choose to write.

One of our activities before reading is to make a list of vocabulary words in our journals. Shai always requires a lot of assistance. I write the words and she traces over the letters. This week, I didn't get to Shai right away. I turned around to find her very carefully trying to write the words herself. She did it, too! Very well. Normally, her writing is very jumbled and 'squiggly,' so I was shocked to see her writing so clearly. I don't know what prompted this change, but it totally made my day! Naturally, I praised her BIG TIME and the whole group clapped for her! It was a great moment!

—Leah G, co-facilitator, Columbus, Ohio

12. Pick a Letter Game

> ➤ **Description:** A member says a letter. Each member then looks at a page of the story being read and finds a word that starts with that letter. Each member then reads the word out loud and states the initial letter.

> ➤ **Expected outcome:** Members learn to identify letters and scan pages. Members also learn to pronounce the words they identify.

> ➤ **Materials needed:** Each member needs to have access to a book. Some members use a bookmark or ruler to scan the page one line at a time.

> ➤ **Time required:** Five to ten minutes.

13. Let's Build a Sentence

> ➤ **Description:** The facilitator or a member chooses a relevant word from the story, and the group creates a sentence using the word correctly. Everyone then takes a turn using the word correctly in a sentence.

> ➤ **Expected outcome:** Members learn new vocabulary and how to use it in a sentence.

> ➤ **Materials needed:** Story being read.

> ➤ **Time required:** One to five minutes.

14. Learn To Use the Dictionary

> ➤ **Description:** When a member reads an unfamiliar word, the facilitator writes that word down on an index card or small dry erase board. When the member finishes reading, before another person reads, she brings out the dictionary. If she knows how to use the dictionary, she can demonstrate finding the first letter of the word, finding the correct page, and searching for the word. If no one knows how to use the dictionary, then the facilitator demonstrates. Someone reads the word definition to the group. Finally, the group defines the word as it was used in the story. It's also possible to combine this with the "*Build a Word List*" activity (item 10) above and add the new word to the group's list.

> ➤ **Expected outcome:** Members learn to recognize unfamiliar words, how to find a word in a dictionary, and how to create meaning from a sentence.

> ➤ **Materials needed:** The story being read, index cards or small dry erase board, a pen or pencil, and a dictionary (consider using a large print version or a page magnifier).

> ➤ **Time required:** Ten to fifteen minutes.

'Reading isn't merely being able to pronounce the words correctly, a fact that surprises most people. Reading is being able to make sense from the marks on the page. Reading is being able to make the print mean something. Reading is getting the message.' (Fox, M. Reading Magic. 2001)

15. Find a Word

- **Description:** Write a word from a page of the story on an index card or small dry erase board and ask members to find the word on page ___.
- **Expected outcome:** Members learn to recall facts of the story.
- **Materials needed:** The book being read, index cards or small dry erase board.
- **Time required:** Five to ten minutes.

16. Crossword Puzzle

- **Description:** Make an easy crossword puzzle (two to three vertical and horizontal words), using questions about the story as clues. If you have access to a copy machine, each member can work on her own puzzle or you can do it as a group.
- **Expected outcome:** Members learn to recall facts of the story and write or copy the letters of the words. Discussion about the correct answer occurs often.
- **Materials needed:** Paper, pen or pencil, and the book being read.
- **Time required:** Twenty to thirty minutes.

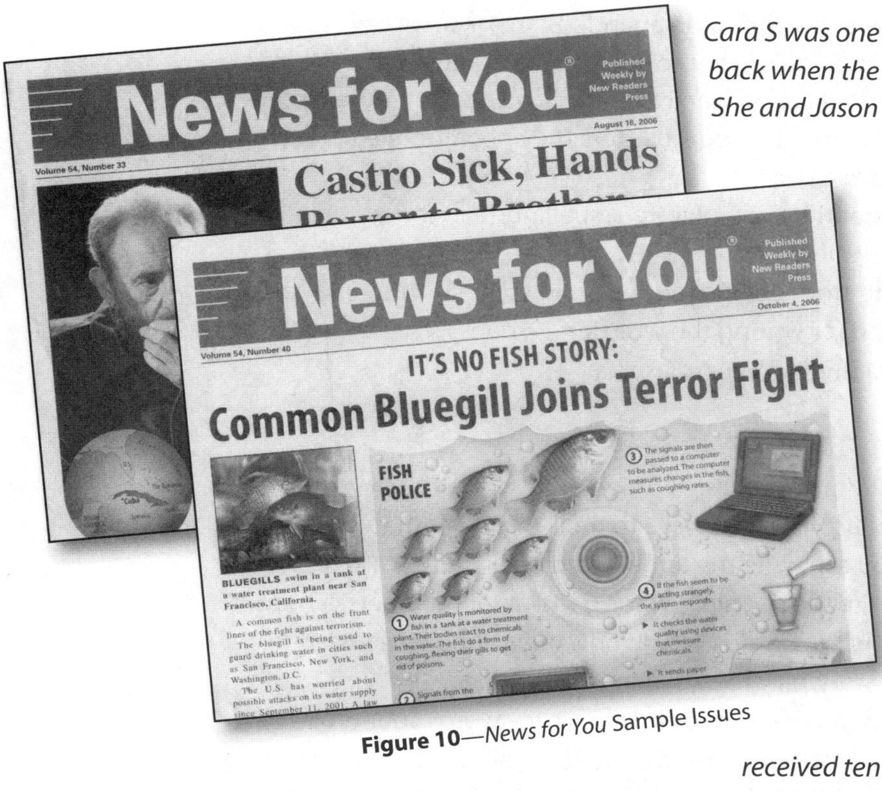
News for You
Published Weekly by New Readers Press
August 16, 2006
Volume 54, Number 33
Castro Sick, Hands

News for You
Published Weekly by New Readers Press
October 4, 2006
Volume 54, Number 40
IT'S NO FISH STORY:
Common Bluegill Joins Terror Fight
FISH POLICE
BLUEGILLS swim in a tank at a water treatment plant near San Francisco, California.
A common fish is on the front lines of the fight against terrorism. The bluegill is being used to guard drinking water in cities such as San Francisco, New York, and Washington, D.C.
The U.S. has worried about possible attacks on its water supply since September 11, 2001. A law

Figure 10—*News for You Sample Issues*

Cara S was one of the first NCBC facilitators back when the program began in 2002. She and Jason W recently got married and requested that in lieu of wedding gifts, invitees consider making a donation to the OSU Nisonger Center to support the Next Chapter Book Club! Thanks to Cara's and Jason's thoughtfulness and the generosity of their family and friends, we subscribed to a newspaper called News for You®, published weekly by New Readers Press, at the classroom rate. Each Columbus club received ten copies for sixteen weeks. The package included a Teacher's Guide with vocabulary, tips before reading the stories, and discussion questions. Some groups found it helpful for some members to read a story or do a puzzle while other members were busy with some other activity.

—Vicki G, program manager, Columbus, Ohio

17. Vertical Name Game

➤ **Description:** Ask each member to write her name on an index card vertically, with each letter directly under the previous letter. Next, ask her to find and write down a word from the book that starts with each letter from their name.

➤ **Expected outcome:** Members learn to attend to letters, to write new words, and members' names.

➤ **Materials needed:** Index cards, pens or pencils, and book being read.

➤ **Time required:** Ten to twenty minutes.

For Members Who Are Readers: Activities To Increase Phonemic Awareness

18. Share Your Letters

➤ **Description:** The facilitator writes five copies of each letter of the alphabet on individual index cards (or you can use any pre-made letters). Each member gets eight to ten different letter cards. Someone selects a word or name from the story and writes it on an index card or small dry erase board; members then provide the appropriate cards or letters to spell the word as a group. A variation on this activity is to have each member spell the word individually. Members request letters they need from each other until they have spelled the word.

➤ **Expected outcome:** Identification of letters, spelling, learning to request, and to respond to questions.

➤ **Materials needed:** The story being read, letters in some form, index cards or small dry erase board for writing the word, and a pen.

➤ **Time required:** Ten to fifteen minutes.

19. Rhyming Game

➤ **Description:** The facilitator identifies recurring words from the story that could be used for rhyming. Members have to think of a word that sounds like the target word. You can write the target word on an index card or small dry erase board and write the rhyming words under it (or members can, on their own cards) to show how words vary in only one sound. Whenever this word reappears in the story, play the Rhyming Game again.

➤ **Expected outcome:** Members learn to listen to how words sound, to identify letters that make specific sounds, and to recall words they know.

➤ **Materials needed:** The story being read, index cards or small dry erase board, pen or pencil.

➤ **Time required:** Five to ten minutes.

➤ **Note:** Sometimes members do not understand the concept of rhyming. But they can usually participate once you start the game.

20. Same First Sound Game

➤ **Description:** The facilitator and members identify the first sound of an important word in the story. A group member writes the word on an index card or small dry erase board, and the facilitator underlines the letter(s) that make the first sound. The facilitator can draw a line down the middle of the index card or board, dividing it in half. She then writes the first sound on the left side of the card and puts the rest of the word on the right side. This will help members understand the concept of first. Once everyone knows the initial sound (not the letter), each person comes up with a word that starts with that sound.

➤ **Expected outcome:** Members learn to identify sounds in words and repeat words that start with the same sound.

➤ **Materials needed:** Story being read, index cards or small dry erase board, pens or pencils.

➤ **Time required:** Ten to fifteen minutes.

21. Same Final Sound Game

➤ **Description:** The facilitator or members identify the last sound of an important word in the story. A group member writes the word on an index card or small dry erase board, and the facilitator underlines the letter(s) that make the final sound. The facilitator can draw a line down the middle of the index card or board, dividing it in half. She then writes all but the final sound on the left of the card and puts the final sound on the right. This will help members understand the concept of last.

➤ **Expected outcome:** Members learn to identify sounds in words and learn the concept of word beginning and ending.

➤ **Materials needed:** Story being read, index cards or small dry erase board, pens or pencils.

➤ **Time required:** Ten to fifteen minutes.

22. Sound Beats in Words

➤ **Description:** The facilitator chooses a word from the story that has two or more syllables, and taps the syllables on the table as she says the word aloud. She chooses a second word and says the word out loud to the group, then asks how many syllables, or "beats," the word has. If the members correctly identify the number of beats, continue the exercise for two or three words. If they are incorrect, the facilitator should back up to tapping the beats on the table as she says the word.

➤ **Expected outcome:** Members will correctly identify the number of syllables in a word.

➤ **Materials needed:** None.

➤ **Time required:** Five to ten minutes.

For Members Who Are Emergent Readers: Activities To Increase Participation and Fluency

To honor our commitment to be an inclusive club, we have developed several literacy activities for our members who have emergent literacy skills. These are often the members who most desire to improve their literacy skills. We try to consider the total literacy environment to support their learning. For example, although a member may not be able to read conventionally, with the social support of members, she may be an active literacy participant.

> *Roy is an interesting case of someone who can't recognize many words yet feels that he is 'reading' and clearly values his relationship with the book and the club. So while he is still not technically literate, he is definitely enjoying a literacy activity that is meaning-ful for him.*   —*Vicki G, program manager and co-facilitator, Columbus, Ohio*

23. Echo-Echo-Echo Reading

> ➤ **Description:** Echo reading is one way members who do not read can actively participate in the group. The facilitator or a fluent reader should sit beside the member. The reader points to a word as she reads it and encour-ages the member to point to the word too. The reader says the first word and pauses, waiting for the member to repeat the word. Once the member is echoing single words easily, increase the unit of reading to phrases. Also, encourage members to try smaller, familiar, or repetitive words on their own. We have found that some members are easily frustrated when asked to "sound a word out," and this can be a difficult skill to teach. Because the pace of echo reading is slow, we tend to limit the amount of echoed read-ing to about a paragraph or alternate it with more fluent reading, so that members maintain their interest and focus on the activity.
> ➤ **Expected outcome:** Increased participation of nonfluent readers; im-proved recognition of sight words.
> ➤ **Materials needed:** Book being read, bookmark or ruler to follow reading.
> ➤ **Time required:** No more than five minutes per member.

> *I know you taught us that the point was 'reading to learn' not 'learning to read,' but I hope you don't mind that reading levels have skyrocketed!!! For several of our partici-pants, the echo reading has just about faded away. For one participant, who would just 'unh' along behind each word, the enunciation level has increased and he actually is reading the words 'the,' 'a,' and 'I' ahead of his helper.*
> —*Nann M, program coordinator and co-facilitator, Monroe, Louisiana*

24. Listen Up and Follow Along

> ➤ **Description:** Members use a piece of folded paper, bookmark, index card, small ruler, etc. to scroll the page as they follow along with the oral reader. Be sure a verbal cue is given when it's time to turn the page.

➤ **Expected outcome:** Members are part of the group activity; learn about concepts of print and how to handle a book.
➤ **Materials needed:** The book being read, a straight edge to follow the text.
➤ **Time required:** Encourage members to follow along whenever someone is reading.

In the young adult club, we have been very excited to watch a member who was a non-reader evolve into someone who could follow along and not lose his place, then a person who wanted to read and had to be told every word, then begin to recognize the recurring names in the story, and lately, to read commonly recurring words independently.
—Sarajane A, program coordinator, Champaign, Illinois

25. Jot It Down

➤ **Description:** Encourage members to draw pictures from their memory of the book or copy words or letters from the story. One member can write words lightly on paper or index cards for others to trace. Members can copy single letters, recurring words, or even doodles, as they are able.
➤ **Expected outcome:** This is a means to adapt writing activities so all members have an opportunity to participate in some way. Drawing, doodling, and copying allow members with fewer skills to be part of the activity and to learn writing skills at their level.
➤ **Materials needed:** All kinds of writing instruments and markers in addition to different kinds of paper will encourage creativity and participation.
➤ **Time required:** Fifteen to thirty minutes.

'[T]rying to write is one of the fastest ways children [and adults] teach themselves to read.' (Fox, M. Reading Magic. 2001)

26. Picture This

➤ **Description:** Ask each member to picture in their mind (or draw a picture of) a scene from the story and then describe it to the group. Encourage other members to ask questions or make comments about the scene or event described.
➤ **Expected outcome:** Members learn to organize their thoughts and communicate an idea to the group. This activity also can help with memory skills and learning to talk on a topic.
➤ **Materials needed:** The book being read, paper with pencils or pens (if members choose to draw what they are picturing).
➤ **Time required:** Fifteen to thirty minutes.

Although having the ability to read is a trait most people want and need, those that cannot read can still gain so much from a book by discussing ideas, talking with others, etc.
—Melissa F, co-facilitator, Columbus, Ohio

27. Find the Letters

➤ **Description:** Have one member identify the first letter of the first word on a page and then read that word (with help). Have another member identify the last letter of the last word on the page and then read that word (with help).

➤ **Expected outcome:** Members learn alphabetic and page orientation skills such as first word/last word, beginning letter of a word.

➤ **Materials needed:** Book being read.

➤ **Time required:** Two to three minutes.

28. Point to It

➤ **Description:** Illustrations are an excellent way to engage nonreaders. Call the group's attention to pictures in the book and ask open-ended questions such as, "What is happening in this picture?" or more specific ones, like, "Can you point to the mouse on the motorcycle?"

➤ **Expected outcome:** Members are part of the group activity and learn to relate the picture to the story. This activity also can help with memory skills and build vocabulary.

➤ **Materials needed:** The book being read.

➤ **Time required:** One to two minutes.

'The pictures tell a thousand words and help unlock the action of the story.' (Fox, M. Reading Magic. 2001)

Strategies and Activities That Encourage Social Interaction

The social context of the book club is a critical component of our success. We actively foster supportive literacy communities where members can participate as much or as little as they choose. Creating a comfortable social space requires that the facilitator knows how to motivate members to engage with one another.

29. Know Each Other's Names

➤ **Description:** One of the first steps to becoming friendly with another person is to know (and remember) that person's name. We may use name tags or write names on index cards, practice repeating each member's name, or create games, like the one below, to help remember each other's name.

➤ **Expected outcome:** Each member will remember the name of people in her club, which encourages better inter-group communication.

➤ **Materials needed:** Name tags, index cards, pens, and markers.

➤ **Time required:** From a few minutes to ten minutes.

30. Names That Sound the Same (also a phonemic awareness activity)

➤ **Description:** This activity helps members learn each other's names and is a phonological awareness activity as well. (Note: Some names are easier to rhyme than others.) The facilitator chooses a person and writes her name on an index card or small dry erase board. The card or board is held facing out in front of the person so members can see how it is spelled. Other members are asked to think of a word that rhymes with the name and the facilitator writes the word to show all the members. Depending on how much time the group would like to spend, you can go around the table and do the same with everyone's name.

➤ **Expected outcome:** Members learn each others' names; they learn to listen to how words sound, and to see how words are spelled.

➤ **Materials needed:** Index card or small dry erase board, pens or markers.

➤ **Time required:** Five minutes per member.

31. Who's Wearing Red?

➤ **Description:** This is another fun way to learn members' names. The facilitator comments on a member's unique article of clothing or aspect of clothing (such as a red shirt, Cleveland Browns shirt, or one with oversized buttons on it) and asks members to identify that person. Once identified, members can write the person's name and identifying characteristic of her clothing on an index card. Note: Be careful about calling attention to a member's personal physical characteristics. If you have members with visual impairments, you can target unique aspects of a person's voice or speech mannerisms to identify.

➤ **Expected outcome:** Members learn someone's name, how to attend to details, and how to write about those observed details.

➤ **Materials needed:** Index cards, markers or pens.

➤ **Time required:** Ten to fifteen minutes.

32. Give It a Try

➤ **Description:** The facilitator and members can invite others to participate in the interaction by directing a comment to specific members and waiting for a response. This is a strategy we like to use to encourage all members to be active in the group. For example, "Jane, would you like to try this sentence with me?"

➤ **Expected outcome:** Increased member participation in the interaction around the book. (It is important to remember that nonverbal participation is as important as verbal participation.)

➤ **Materials needed:** Awareness of the participation patterns of individuals in the club.

➤ **Time required:** One to five minutes or more.

33. NCBC Scrabble®

➤ **Description:** The facilitator places a Scrabble game on the table and divides the tiles among the members. One member chooses a word from the book to start the game. The facilitator writes the word on an index card or small dry erase board, so that each member can see the word. One person places a tile with the first letter of the word on the center of the game board and turns to the player on her left to place the second letter, etc. until the word is completed. Another word is chosen that will intersect with the first word and the game is repeated. To stimulate social interaction, it's helpful to require that members work together.

➤ **Expected outcome:** Members must ask each other if she has the next letter, discuss the next word, and help each other look for letters.

➤ **Materials needed:** The book being read, a Scrabble game with extra tiles if possible, index cards or small dry erase board, pen or pencil.

➤ **Time required:** Fifteen to thirty minutes.

34. Comments Only

➤ **Description:** Oftentimes, questions tend to close rather than open conversations. One activity facilitators use to open conversational exchange is to comment on something that was read or said and then wait. We can teach this conversational strategy to members in the group and practice using the strategy. As positive reinforcement, when a member comments, she gets a "high five" from the group.

➤ **Expected outcome:** Longer conversational exchanges on topics of interest to the members.

➤ **Materials needed:** None.

➤ **Time required:** It may take a few practice sessions for members to learn and demonstrate the activity; once they have it, the activity takes one to two minutes.

35. Let's Get Started

➤ **Description:** It's important that all members take an active role in creating the club. Think of how nonreading members might assist the club. The member might arrive early to help move tables and chairs together for the club, or carry a drink to the table.

➤ **Expected outcome:** All members take ownership for the club and feel responsible to each other.

➤ **Materials needed:** None.

➤ **Time required:** Two to three minutes.

36. Members Helping Members

➤ **Description:** Often members have had limited experiences helping others. Although each club is different, we often have members with a spectrum of skills. The facilitators can help members capitalize on their personal skills by coaching them to help other members with reading, turning a page, making a comment, taking a turn, etc. Sometimes "buddy" pairs form naturally, where a member with strong skills matches up with a member with weaker skills.

➤ **Expected outcome:** Members become more responsive to each other and may start to develop friendships.

➤ **Materials needed:** None.

➤ **Time required:** The facilitator may need to coach members on how to help each other, and this may take several practice opportunities. Once the activity of helping is learned, it can take less than a minute to do.

37. Things in Common

➤ **Description:** Facilitators often learn about the members' interests. They can encourage members with similar interests to share them with the group or to develop their mutual interests further in a small group or pair.

➤ **Expected outcome:** Increased opportunities for developing mutual conversations and for friendships.

➤ **Materials needed:** Knowledge of members' interests and activities outside of the club.

➤ **Time required:** A few minutes during the club, but we also encourage meetings before or after the club (or between meetings).

KC's mother called today to express how much KC enjoyed Book Club. She told her mom that it was the first time she actually felt like she belonged in a group. She was so comfortable being with our group. She cannot wait to participate every Wednesday and wishes she could come more often!

—Tory H, program coordinator and co-facilitator, Port Clinton, Ohio

38. Start a Phone Tree

➤ **Description:** Ask each member if she would like to share her phone number and participate in phone calls with other club members between club meetings. Write the names and phone numbers of all who want to participate on a piece paper and make a copy for each participating member. Each week, explain what a phone tree is, where the first person calls one or two people, then they each call one or two people, and they each call one or two people. Discuss when appropriate calling times might be. Facilitators can begin the phone tree with a few questions each member can ask the next, such as, "What are you doing this weekend?"

➤ **Expected outcome:** Members learn to use the telephone, follow appropriate etiquette, and may develop outside friendships.

➤ **Materials needed:** Phone list with members' names; access to a telephone.

➤ **Time required:** Ten to fifteen minutes.

39. Memories and Current Events (Holidays, etc.)

➤ **Description:** We have found that members enjoy discussing current events, their holiday traditions and plans, and special community events (in Columbus, Ohio, it is OSU football). We encourage members to bring in and share with others their memories around a photograph, some memorabilia, or a card ("print artifact"). This can then be developed into a recurring activity at the beginning or end of meetings. Sometimes members can hardly wait to share a current event, in which case sharing would come first. We might shift into a literacy activity incorporating this event (such as drawing a football with the score of the last game on it) to intertwine the social, literacy, and community components.

➤ **Expected outcome:** Members share their experiences and memories with interested listeners, and they relate these experiences to a "print artifact."

➤ **Materials needed:** Print artifact from a member's life to share with the group.

➤ **Time required:** Varies; this can take five to ten minutes, or it could be planned to take the whole hour. Remember, the goal is not reading per se but reading, social interaction, and community inclusion combined.

It has been exciting to watch these young people learn to take part in a small group discussion and to then use that skill in other settings.

—Sarajane A, program coordinator, Champaign, Illinois

40. Celebrate Birthdays

➤ **Description:** The facilitator makes a note of all birthdays for members, facilitators, and friends at the host site (if appropriate) each month. All members can make a card and extend birthday greetings. Gift-giving is not encouraged, but special literacy or social activities often take place on birthdays.

➤ **Expected outcome:** Members learn to appreciate and acknowledge the special interests of others. They learn literacy skills while making cards and social skills when interacting with the member or other person who has a birthday.

➤ **Materials needed:** Construction paper, markers, and calendar to keep track of birthdays.

➤ **Time required:** Fifteen minutes.

41. Autobiographies

➤ **Description:** Members create a list of biographical questions that everyone will answer. (Groups have used questions similar to these: Where were you born? What is your favorite food? Where did you go on your last vacation?) Members can take the questions home and discuss with family or support staff and then bring the answers back the following week. Members might choose to write out their responses or jot down notes to help remember what to talk about.

➤ **Expected outcome:** Members recreate their own histories, organize how they will tell about themselves, and then share with the group. Note: The person who makes the reminder phone calls can remind members that biographies will be discussed.

➤ **Materials needed:** Paper, pens, markers.

➤ **Time required:** The prep activity takes ten to fifteen minutes; the sharing can take fifteen to thirty minutes.

42. NCBC Superstars

➤ **Description:** The facilitator creates a short form with two or three questions (such as, What's your favorite restaurant? or Where did you go on vacation last?) to help members get to know each other and learn how to talk about themselves and interact with others. Each week, one member takes the form home, completes it (family or staff can help if needed) and then brings it back the following week to share with the group and be the "superstar" for the day.

➤ **Expected outcome:** Each member thinks about what she wants to share with the group (support staff or family can be included at member's request). The club gets to learn something new about that member and perhaps find common interests.

➤ **Materials needed:** Paper or index cards and pen or pencil to complete the form.

➤ **Time required:** Five to ten minutes.

43. To Your Neighbor

➤ **Description:** Ask each member to turn to a person seated next to her and tell that person about a character or event from the book that she liked or enjoyed.

➤ **Expected outcome:** Members learn to talk about the book in a one-to-one situation.

➤ **Materials needed:** None.

➤ **Time required:** Five to ten minutes.

44. Has That Ever Happened to You?

➤ **Description:** The facilitator asks members how the story relates to *their* lives. For example: "Have you ever been in a tornado like Dorothy? Who do you go to when you need help?" Learning how to relate what they read in books to their own lives is a powerful learning tool. Facilitators may need to help members make that connection at first and then back off once members get the idea.

➤ **Expected outcome:** Members learn how "stories" relate to their own lives and what we might learn from the story.

➤ **Time required:** This can take five to twenty minutes, depending on the story and the members.

45. Theme Week

➤ **Description:** Holidays, current events, or an event in the book might inspire a theme for the week. Members and facilitators might dress as a favorite character, bring articles or memorabilia to the club, or discuss particular themes. For example, if a character from a book has to do chores, members might discuss the chores they have to do at home and whether they enjoy doing chores.

➤ **Expected outcome:** Members extend the book club activities to their home life and take responsibility for facilitating parts of the discussion.

➤ **Materials needed:** Varies, depending on the theme.

➤ **Time required:** Thirty minutes to the entire hour.

46. What Would That Be Like?

➤ **Description:** At selected times when reading the book, pause to discuss with members what they think it might be like to be in the situation of the character. For example: "What would it be like to fly like Peter Pan?"

➤ **Expected outcome:** Members learn to relate the book to their own life and experiences and learn to discuss ideas and feelings.

➤ **Materials needed:** The book being read.

➤ **Time required:** Fifteen to thirty minutes.

To promote social interactions, we carried out a few activities related to the books we were reading. For 'Around the World in 80 Days,' we used a map to track the journey. For 'Nancy Drew,' we gave the members a mystery to solve. We put six items in a box and asked the members to guess what they were by asking questions.

—Charu A, co-facilitator, Gahanna, Ohio

47. What's In the Bag?

➤ **Description:** As part of all NCBC trainings, affiliates receive NCBC book bags for all members and facilitators in the first club. Additional bags are available for purchase from the NCBC Central Office. For this activity, the facilitator pulls out various materials from her NCBC bag at strategic points throughout the book club meeting to share items that will spark discussions and social interaction related to the story. For example, if the book talks about types of clothing, you could pull out a hat similar to the style mentioned in the story and give everyone a chance to try it on. The key is that each item pulled out of the bag should be connected to the story being read at the meeting. Members can take charge of this activity by bringing something in their bag to the meeting that relates to the story and describing it to the others.

➤ **Expected outcome:** Members learn to remain focused on the story and discussion through their curiosity about what else will be coming out of the bag. Members can practice and improve social interaction and conversational skills.

➤ **Materials needed:** The book being read and various items brought from outside.

➤ **Time required:** Fifteen to thirty minutes, or the entire hour.

48. A Time to Share

➤ **Description:** Monthly, the facilitators ask one or two members to disclose something new about themselves to the group.

➤ **Expected outcome:** Members learn more about each other, learn to have a conversation on a topic of interest to someone else, and learn helpful conversational strategies to make friends.

➤ **Materials needed:** None.

➤ **Time required:** Five to ten minutes.

While visiting one of our Columbus clubs, I learned that Laura, one of the members, was teaching the rest of the group American Sign Language! She had created two notebooks with illustrations of each sign and sample sentences. The facilitators offered members the option to read their book or do sign language for that meeting. They voted for ASL and split into two smaller groups to practice.
—Vicki G, program manager, Columbus, Ohio

49. Choose the Next Book

➤ **Description:** The facilitator guides the members in a decision-making process to choose which book the club will read next. This might consist of a verbal discussion followed by voting on a paper ballot. As a club approaches finishing a book, the facilitator will contact the program coordinator to determine which books might be available from the NCBC library. The PC sends the facilitator a list with a short description of each book. For example: This is a story about a family who lived and worked on a farm before there were cars and trucks. Facilitators can make suggestions and add a potential book selection to the list of possibilities; we also encourage members to bring in their own suggested book titles. However, most clubs vote on which book to read based on those available.

➤ **Expected outcome:** Members learn to assert themselves, compromise within the group, how to cast a vote, and how to go along with majority rule.

➤ **Materials needed:** A list of available books, paper, pens or pencils.

➤ **Time required:** This process typically takes a whole hour.

Many of our literacy and social interaction activities facilitate multiple outcomes. For example, a literary discussion of something that happened in a story can easily foster social interaction, as members reveal things they know or care about. Although we sometimes focus on improving one skill, more typically we use these activities to engage members, switching from one activity to another to keep everyone actively involved and interested.

> *Sometimes the new members would be nervous, so I would always encourage them to read a short poem or something that would at least involve speaking with others. That always seemed to work, as many members who were once the quietest became quite comfortable and therefore vocal!*
>
> —*Amber M, co-facilitator, Gahanna, Ohio*

Strategies and Activities That Increase Community Inclusion

> *Adam once said, 'It's nice to feel like a normal person just hanging out.'*
>
> —*Mark F, co-facilitator, Columbus, Ohio*

The NCBC represents a very real step for and towards community inclusion. From inception, we've been unyielding in our assertion that clubs would meet in bookstores and cafés located in communities. Isolated meeting places, shut off from mainstream community activities, were never considered an appropriate setting. While a church, for example, might be centrally located and may be a hub of activities, our clubs would most likely meet in a closed room. The NCBCs are not about meeting behind closed doors. Even if we were to meet in an open fellowship hall, there would still be an element of separation, as a church is not a crossroads of community activity for all.

Does holding a book club once a week in a bookstore or café assure that someone with a disability, who is an NCBC member, will feel included in her community? Of course not, but we know it is often difficult to translate community inclusion into daily life. NCBC is one activity that seamlessly integrates people with ID, so that they might form regular relationships within their communities.

There are a number of strategies that NCBC facilitators can use to increase community inclusion for NCBC members. We encourage facilitators to use their own creativity to develop authentic and ongoing community inclusion for and with book club members. We have learned that NCBC members know more than people give them credit for and have wonderful ideas and opinions—if we only ask them.

> *Our career and technical school students love belonging to a book club and being out in the community. As I have visited them in the classroom, I see that they also spend time in the classroom reading. We have seen an improvement in reading skills, and for our one 'nontalker,' it is obvious that he understands and enjoys being a part of this adult activity.*
>
> —*Mary L, program coordinator and assistant principal, Ft. Wayne, Indiana*

50. Explore Your Host Site

➤ **Description:** Take a trip through your host site. If your club meets in a book-store, ask members, "If you could read about anything, what would it be?" Then help them find books about the selected topics. If your club meets in a coffee shop, ask the manager for a "behind-the-scenes" tour of the facility.

➤ **Expected outcome:** Increased social connections, skill development, and community participation. Better appreciation and understanding of resources in the host site.

➤ **Materials needed:** None.

➤ **Time required:** Maybe fifteen to thirty minutes or the entire hour, as desired.

51. Off To the Library We Go

➤ **Description:** Take your members to the library and teach them how to understand and use their local library. You'll need to send a letter in advance or make prior arrangements with each member to provide transportation (for that day) to the local library. Typically support staff or family members will drop members off at the library, where facilitators will be waiting. If any members want to get a library card, they'll need to bring proper identification (and may need a guardian to accompany them). You may also want to include a discussion about other sources for inexpensive books, such as yard sales, half-priced bookstores, and borrowing from friends. You can even discuss setting up an informal lending library among the group. (Be sure to announce the meeting time and place to families or support staff and include this information in your weekly reminder phone call.)

➤ **Expected outcome:** Members will learn how to understand and use their local library and other sources for inexpensive books.

➤ **Materials needed:** At least one facilitator should have a library card to demonstrate how to check out books.

➤ **Time required:** Plan to use the entire hour.

52. Let's Take a Field Trip

➤ **Description:** This activity typically takes place after reading a book and often includes walking to an area store or activity. If transportation beyond the immediate vicinity of the book club is required, you should notify the members' support staff or families in writing well in advance of the activity. Halfway though the book, facilitators should encourage members to think about where they may want to go after they finish the book. For example,

If your club is reading...	You might want to visit...
Peter Pan	an airport
The Adventures of Robin Hood	a forest
The Adventures of Huckleberry Finn	a riverboat ride
The Story of Dr. Dolittle	a zoo or farm

➤ **Expected outcome:** Members have a real-life experience that relates directly to the book they've just read. They also enjoy an activity together in a community setting.

➤ **Materials needed:** Pictures of where the event will take place and/or a written description. Generally we do not recommend that family members and/or support staff join the activity, to maintain the member's independence and the group character of the event. However, if a member needs assistance beyond what facilitators can accommodate, and/or if the nature of the event requires close supervision, then we would welcome assistance from staff or family.

➤ **Time required:** We recommend from one and a half to two hours. More time would probably require significant arrangements for members and facilitators beyond the scope of NCBC.

We are reading 'Phantom Victory,' a book that is set at Put in Bay, Ohio. We are going to take a trip to Put in Bay to read the last chapter and find the Victory Hotel when we get to the last chapter.

—Tory H, program coordinator and co-facilitator, Port Clinton, Ohio

53. What Did You Do This Week?

➤ **Description:** Each person in the club, including facilitators, is encouraged to share one good and one not-so-good thing they did or that happened to them over the past week. The emphasis should be on community-based experiences and activities even though this may initially be a challenge. The rules are that you cannot say such things as "nothing" or "same old thing."

➤ **Expected outcome:** Members will learn to think about what they did before coming to their club. They may also get to know one another better and practice their communication skills.

➤ **Materials needed:** Members may want to have a small notebook or notepad to write down what they want to say.

➤ **Time required:** Two to three minutes for each person.

54. Read Weekend Section of the Newspaper

➤ **Description:** Most local newspapers have a section that appears on Thursdays or Fridays and details upcoming weekend events and activities. These might include shows, exhibits, festivals, and other entertainment. Facilitators can bring this section of the newspaper to the meeting or ask for a member to volunteer to do so. Members then take turns reading about upcoming weekend activities that might be of interest.

➤ **Expected outcome:** Better awareness of what is going on in the community and what activities interest other members. This activity may also lead to group outings and cultivate friendships.

➤ **Materials needed:** A local newspaper.

➤ **Time required:** About fifteen minutes once a month at the start of the weekly NCBC meeting.

55. Make an Address Book

➤ **Description:** This activity involves both reading and writing in helping members to purchase, set up, maintain, and use an address book. Facilitators will lead a discussion of the activity, including the rationale behind it, initial member responses to the idea, and group suggestions about where, when, and how to purchase the address books. (If you decide to shop together for address books, either where you meet for weekly sessions or somewhere else in the community, be sure to announce the meeting time and place to families or support staff and include this information in the weekly reminder phone calls.) Once they have purchased their books, members should bring them to club the following week to start entering addresses and phone numbers of fellow members. They may also wish to decorate the covers with personal art or perhaps the NCBC logo.

➤ **Expected outcome:** Members will have a systematic way of more independently contacting friends, family, service providers, resources in the community, etc. Members will have an enduring resource for developing an information and support network. By keeping addresses, phone numbers, possibly emails, and any other resource information, members will be able to retrieve who and what they know.

➤ **Materials needed:** Members need to bring money. We recommend buying books that are simple, allow for plenty of information, and have an age-appropriate appearance. Members can decide whether they all want the same books or different ones.

➤ **Time required:** Fifteen to twenty minutes for initial discussion of the activity; fifteen to thirty minutes to purchase address books, depending on where it happens; ten to fifteen minutes to decorate the covers, if desired; twenty to thirty minutes to start the process of entering addresses and phone numbers. These times are spread over three or more weeks. Then, about once a month, members may bring in their address books and share something about a person, service, or activity listed in their books for five to ten minutes.

56. Draw Your Dream Home or Apartment

➤ **Description:** All club members, including facilitators, draw the home of their dreams along with a visual pathway of the neighborhood where it would be located. For example, a member might want to live by the beach; she might draw her dream house overlooking the ocean with large windows, a boat, and kites. The actual drawing is not as important as their description of the house or apartment and the neighborhood where it is located. We encourage discussion about the types of neighbors they would want. What makes a good neighbor? Written description (of any kind) on the back of the drawing will help members remember what they want to say.

➤ **Expected outcome:** Members will begin to think more about where they might want to live. They should also develop a better sense of what a neighborhood consists of and what it takes to be a good neighbor.

➤ **Materials needed:** Oversized white construction paper or butcher paper, crayons or colored felt pens.

➤ **Time required:** About twenty to thirty minutes each week for two or three consecutive weeks including drawings, individual presentations, and group discussion.

57. See the City or Town

➤ **Description:** Members identify locations in their community using a map, such as the street where they live, locations where they work or go for program services, and fun places, like movie theaters, parks, and recreation centers. Each week, for as many consecutive weeks as there are members, club members take turns identifying the location they want to find and then marking it with a different colored pin or sticker on a local map. They then talk about those places, including the following:

  - what they like about the place;
  - how they get to and from there;
  - what kind of buildings and people are nearby; and
  - when they are going there next.

➤ **Expected outcome:** A better visual awareness of where things are located in the community. Better understanding of how to get from place to place. Also helps members get to know one another better.

➤ **Materials needed:** A local street map would work; however, the more visual symbols on the map, the better. Primary responsibility for securing the map will fall on facilitators, but in discussing this activity, some members may have ideas about where to find a map. Good places to start include the local bookstore, chamber of commerce, or tourism office. We recommend mounting the map on lightweight foam board and using colored stick pins with large heads that can be easily manipulated.

➤ **Time required:** About ten minutes a week for as many consecutive weeks as there are members and facilitators. We suggest that one member be responsible for bringing the mounted map each week. The club may want to revisit the activity every six months or so; if so, members need to decide who will store the map until the next time it's used.

As our members were arriving Thursday night, one of the staff members at the Target store greeted one of the members and accompanied her to the meeting. This is the second time the two of them have interacted (that I have observed), and the Target employee seems to be particularly interested in our group. It's at least a good sign that NCBC is achieving some of its goals. We're definitely raising awareness and promoting social interaction and inclusion.

—Leah G, co-facilitator, Columbus, Ohio

How Do You Market and Promote the NCBC Program?

13

My wife and I are active recruiters for the NCBC! We believe it's a great opportunity for people with disabilities to have an intellectually stimulating literacy activity as adults.
— Gregory G, parent and legal guardian, Columbus, Ohio

Before we talk about strategies for marketing the NCBC, it's important to consider to whom we are marketing this program. Of course, we have to appeal to individuals with ID and convey the essence of what the clubs are about. However, without understanding, support, and cooperation from families, support staff, and service coordinators, the program would cease to exist. These are the people who sanction what we do. They provide transportation and exert influence, and thus play a crucial role. They are also hugely important as ambassadors for how "cool" the program is. Thus, these are the people we need to reach out to first, and then continue to reinforce how much we appreciate their support and cooperation.

Reaching Out to Families, Support Staff, and Service Coordinators

Here are some things you can do as a facilitator or program coordinator to increase understanding, support, and cooperation from families, support staff, and service coordinators:

- Thank them for bringing the member, e.g., "We really appreciate your taking the time to bring Juan to book club."
- Give them feedback by sharing something specific that the member has said or done, e.g., "Marie took a lot more turns reading tonight and seems very interested in the *Huck Finn* book we're reading."

- Ask how they're doing, e.g., "How are things going? Anything new and exciting?"
- Ask them for advice or suggestions about how to better understand and work with their family member or consumer, such as, "Bill seems a little reluctant to interact with other members. Can you suggest some ways that we can try to draw him out?"
- Let them know things well in advance, like if the club will be cancelled because both facilitators will be out of town. You can do this by phone, by email, in person, or with a written note that members pass along. (We want members to assume as much responsibility as possible.)
- Tell them about the progress of NCBCs across the county to let them know that their family member or consumer is part of a larger network. Suggest that they periodically check out the NCBC website.
- Suggest ways for them to initiate other reading and literacy experiences for the members, such as visits to the library and reading at home, e.g., "Linda really loves to read, and I think she might respond well to verbal encouragement and reinforcement to read at home on a regular basis. What would you think about that?"
- Lastly, and most importantly, be sure to ask parents and support staff what they have observed since their family member or consumer has been in the NCBC. You could ask a question as simple as, "How does Carol like being in the book club?" Then wait for a response, because you are likely to hear some great stories and feedback.

One member, Patrick, is seventeen years old. His father has to beg him to go to basketball, baseball, and Boy Scouts. His mother told me that Patrick loves the book club and it is something he looks forward to every week. She said her husband was not mad. But he could not believe that out of all the stuff he has tried to get Patrick involved in, a book club is the one thing he never thought he would see his son enjoying so much. I thought that was great.

—Sean H, program coordinator and co-facilitator, Sparta, New Jersey

Reaching Out to Service Agencies and Advocacy Organizations

It would prove difficult for me as a government policy maker, social service volunteer, and avid reader to find a more ideal project. NCBC highlights the use of volunteers, it is easy to replicate (for government and nongovernment entities), and it delivers on all of its promises to those it is designed to serve.

—Jeff Davis, former Deputy Director,
Ohio Department of Mental Retardation and Developmental Disabilities

Beyond families, support staff, and service coordinators, it's necessary to market the NCBC to service agencies and advocacy organizations, which can make referrals for facilitators and members. In addition, service agencies and advocacy organizations may be potential affiliates of the NCBC. Here are some effective ways to do this:

- Make presentations at agency staff meetings. Consider taking some members with you to the staff meeting or showing the NCBC promotional video, available from the Central Office.
- Distribute brochures, flyers, and/or posters to disability and literacy programs in your area. Also, consider posting flyers on bulletin boards at local universities, bookstores, coffee shops, and cafés.
- At the staff meetings and other presentations mentioned above, hand out NCBC bookmarks with the website URL on them along with other contact information to key members of service agencies and advocacy organizations.
- Cross-list the NCBC website with other websites.
- Make telephone calls to supervisors at local agencies or organizations and explain the program and its mission. Service coordination and job training supervisors are often good sources of referral.
- Offer to let service agents and advocates contact other agencies or organizations that have become NCBC affiliates in their community for testimony about their experience with the program.
- Advertise the NCBC on websites and listservs. These are also wonderful venues for recruiting prospective members and facilitators.
- Spread the word through newspaper, newsletter, and magazine articles about the NCBC. Our experience has been that these entities are often quite willing to and interested in writing articles about the NCBC.

Congratulations on your article in Exceptional Parent magazine, which reaches a significant percentage of all USA parents with children with disabilities. You have a great program, and you bring positive publicity to Nisonger Center and the University. You are bringing meaningfulness and joy to the lives of a great number of people.

—Steven Reiss, PhD, professor and former Nisonger Center Director

Reaching Out to People with Intellectual Disabilities

Of course, we also need to market the program to individuals with ID. We recommend that prospective members read or have read to them the information about NCBC in Chapter 7. Prospective and current NCBC members should and can be ambassadors for the program. After all, the clubs are for them, and they should play a key role in helping to spread the word. We have found that word-of-mouth endorsements from those interested in joining or those already in clubs are extremely effective. (Nothing tells a story better than hearing it from a friend.)

Here are some useful ways that members can help other people with ID learn about the NCBC:

- Ask current members to tell their friends and co-workers about NCBC.
- Consider offering a small incentive, such as a gift certificate, for each member who recruits a new member. Another option is to pool members' names and conduct a monthly drawing to receive an incentive.

- Suggest that members make presentations at self-advocacy meetings, such as People First.
- Give members brochures, flyers, bookmarks, and/or posters about the program to pass out at their place of employment or other programs.
- Suggest that members invite a friend or co-worker to visit their club.
- Encourage members to carry their NCBC book bags with them and purchase and wear NCBC T-shirts.

Question: What would you suggest changing about your book club?
Answer: 'Spread the news around; tell more people about it.'
—Brian G, member, Columbus, Ohio

How To Approach Funding Sources and Community Organizations

The NCBC is a relatively low-cost program that gives back enormous value to the community. The majority of the cost of running the program is paying the program coordinator, who maintains at least one book club and potentially expands the project. This position may require from two to twenty hours per week. Other potential costs include books, book bags, T-shirts, brochures, pens, markers, dry erase boards, bookmarks, and other promotional materials, as well as adaptive technology such as voice augmentation devices. Some affiliates may cover these costs directly in their budget; others may choose to seek funds from outside sources.

You can use many of the strategies outlined in previous sections of this chapter to market the NCBC to other potential funding sources and generic community organizations, such as libraries and literacy groups. NCBC folders, available for purchase from the Central Office, present our brochure and a variety of other marketing materials contained on our website and elsewhere in this book. NCBC staff can also be helpful in suggesting strategies that have proven successful as well as help to tailor an approach specifically for your situation. Often inviting community representatives to visit a book club or offering them a brief verbal description of NCBC is just the right approach, particularly when pitching the program to a small group of people.

The beauty of the NCBC is that it sort of sells itself. Those who understand and get it usually really understand and get it—almost like a light has gone off in their heads.
—*Tom Fish, program director, Columbus, Ohio*

14 How Can You Evaluate the NCBC Program?

Over the years, we've developed several tools to evaluate Next Chapter Book Clubs and the progress that some of our members have made in literacy skills, social connection, and community inclusion. Evaluation of our clubs has helped us improve and continually develop our book clubs, helped us remain responsive to our members and our communities, and kept us accountable to our funding sources.

One core feature of the evaluation of NCBCs is the inclusion of members in every aspect of evaluation planning, implementation, and analysis. Often, we developed evaluation tools after discussing reports we received from families or support staff regarding the changes they observed in the participating NCBC member. On other occasions, as researchers, we wanted to try to measure the potential effects of the book club on our members' social interaction or literacy participation. We then adapted instruments to gauge subtle social and literacy changes. We also developed evaluation protocols to better serve the varied needs of facilitators and to respond to their questions and concerns in a timely and effective manner.

We describe these tools in this chapter and offer them in the appendices and included CD-ROM for affiliates to use or adapt if they wish. Please contact the NCBC Central Office if you desire more information on how to use them systematically.

Literacy Evaluations

We have adapted and developed two tools to help us better understand and operationally define the literacy skills of members: the Five-Level Scale of Literacy Skills and the ECO-NCBC Literacy Observations. A facilitator completes the **Five-Level Scale of Literacy Skills** (Appendix H) for each member within three weeks from the start of the group. (See Chapter 1 for details.) This instrument helps facilitators understand the literacy decoding and comprehension skills of members. The facilitator rates each member based on her observations of the members' abilities on the following scale:

Level I—no letter recognition or understanding of written language,

Level II—recognizes and understands letters,

Level III—reads and understands single words,

Level IV—reads and understands sentences,

Level V—reads and understands paragraphs.

The Five-Level Scale of Literacy Skills can also be used after completing a book to re-assess a member's skills.

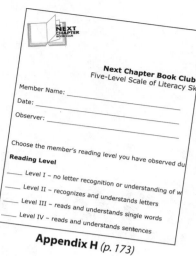

Appendix H (p. 173)

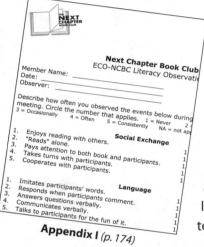

Appendix I (p. 174)

The **ECO-NCBC Literacy Observations** form (Appendix I) is a tool developed to measure a member's interaction, communication, and literacy behaviors within the social context of the NCBC experience. We designed it so that a facilitator or other trained observer can administer it. Typically, the trained facilitator observes a member during a book club meeting and rates her on each question of the ECO-NCBC. Examples include "Pays attention to both book and participants" and "Points to pictures." The instrument uses a five-point Likert scale to assess skills in the areas of social interaction, language, conversation, and literacy. It can be administered periodically to measure targeted competencies for change.

Family Members and Support Staff Evaluations

It has been our experience that book club members often rely on their social supports (family members and support staff) to learn about the program, to provide transportation, and to encourage active participation in the club. Family members frequently report to us that they have observed changes in the member's home literacy activities (she reads signs as we drive now) or social connectedness (she initiates talking more when she is with the family). To help us understand more about the expectations of family members and support staff (and what they were hoping their participating family member might gain from participation in NCBC), we developed the **Family/Staff Expectations Survey** (Appendix J).

This semi-structured interview and rating scale in the three areas of literacy, social interaction, and community inclusion is completed by our book club program coordinators. It allows us to understand some of the expectations that family members and support staff have of the book club by asking questions about the NCBC member's home reading activities and rating the member's satisfaction with her social life and community participation. Often what members do and see at home can be a reflection of what is expected of them. When members see family members reading, interacting, and participating in their communities, this can have a direct ef-

Appendix J (p. 175)

fect on how and what they do in the NCBC club. For this reason, we gather information from the family's perspective on the member's satisfaction with her current literacy, social skills, and community involvement. For example, Dean F told us that his brother Jeff had no peer relationships after moving to Franklin County, Ohio. "Jeff has always been sweet and social" and wanted to make friends. He joined the NCBC mainly for the opportunity for social interaction.

The follow-up to the Family/Staff Expectations Survey is the **Family/Staff Satisfaction Survey** (Appendix K), which family members and support staff complete after the club reads one book (about 12–14 weeks) or other suitable time interval. It consists of rating the member's satisfaction with her literacy, social life, and community participation since joining the NCBC (similar to the Family/Staff Expectations Survey).

Appendix K (p. 177)

Questions for Member Interviews

We use the **Questions for Member Interviews** (Appendix L) to gather marketing data on initial exposure to the NCBC project and to understand each member's perspective about past and current literacy experiences at home and in the workplace. Because members vary widely in their literacy skill level and experiences, we developed this instrument to help us understand what attracted a member to NCBC and what keeps her coming.

The semi-structured interview is completed by the program coordinator and inquires as to members' current home literacy practices, early reading experiences (in school), and current reading experiences at home and in the workplace. It also asks questions about the book a member is currently reading in the book club. This tool is designed to be used with active, current members.

Chuckie's Questionnaire, developed by one of our members and described in Chapter 7, is shown in Appendix M. This is a quick satisfaction survey suitable for one member to ask of other members. It also lets the members know that one of their peers is interested in how they're doing and what they need. Local affiliates may adapt and revise it as they wish.

Appendix L (p. 180)

Appendix M (p. 182)

Questions for Facilitator Interviews

In all of our book clubs, facilitators volunteer their time and bring a wealth of information and expertise. The **Questions for Facilitator Interviews** survey (Appendix N), completed by the program coordinator or submitted by the facilitator, has two main outcomes: 1) It helps evaluate and improve the effectiveness of facilitator training, and 2) It expands the repertoire of activities that promote literacy, social interaction, and community participation. Early in the project we recognized that NCBC facilitators brought exceptional talent, energy, and commitment to the club. This instrument allows us to continually develop and share facilitator-generated ideas among the group of facilitators. We also feature ideas elicited from these interviews in this book, on our website, and during our training sessions. This interview may be conducted anytime during a facilitator's service to the NCBC. It is also helpful to use as an exit interview to capture the facilitators' impressions after they leave.

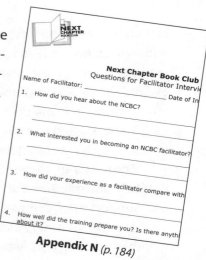

Appendix N (p. 184)

Community Inclusion Surveys

We developed the **Community Inclusion Surveys** (Appendices O and P) as a way to measure a member's level of integration within her community when she initially joined an NCBC and after twelve or more weeks of participation in the book club. As community participation is a primary component of the model, we want to describe the initial community inclusion experiences of the current members and to note changes or improvements over time in members' community participation. We suggest that the **Community Inclusion Survey for Members BEFORE Book Club** (Appendix O) be given prior to a member's enrollment in a club. The **Community Inclusion-Location Survey for Members AFTER Book Club** (Appendix P) may be given after twelve weeks, six months, or one year of membership in a club.

Also, because we are interested in the social context of community inclusion, we want to better understand the beliefs and attitudes of employees working in the cafés and coffee shops toward individuals with intellectual disabilities. We modified the **Community Living Attitudes Scale** (Henry et al., 1999) (Appendix Q) to administer it to the primary, recurring service personnel in the places where the clubs meet. We are interested not only in attitudes from the members' perspectives but also in the perspectives of the larger "community" in which clubs meet regularly.

Appendix O (p. 186)

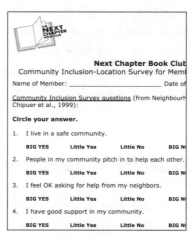

Appendix P (p. 189)

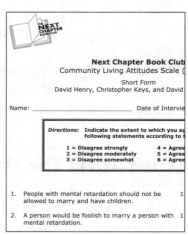

Appendix Q (p. 193)

I had a great chat with the staff about their impressions of our book club that meets in the Barnes & Noble café on Fridays. They have developed a personal relationship with a number of our members; they know many by name and know what they usually order. One staff person named Joanna told me that she looks forward to seeing each member when they come in on Fridays. The great thing about this, in my opinion, is that the staff treats our members with the same 'legendary' service that they treat all Starbucks customers. Two staff people, who were not working that day, happened to be at the café and greeted several members of the club and engaged them in conversation after our meeting.

—Jeff S, co-facilitator, Columbus, Ohio

We understand that many affiliates do not have the staff, resources, or interest to conduct evaluations using the tools we describe in this chapter. We've made them as simple to use as possible. If you would like more information about how to use them systematically to evaluate and improve your book club program, please contact the NCBC Central Office.

15 CONCLUSION: What's the Next Chapter?

Participation in the Next Chapter Book Club provides opportunities for all involved to learn, make friends, and become involved in their communities. Learning is an ongoing process and one to which people with disabilities should be afforded equal access. Next Chapter Book Clubs promote literacy learning in an accessible and socially inclusive manner.

But we know we can do more. Affiliate organizations around the country and beyond are already expanding the potential of the NCBC model beyond our expectations. Here are some examples:

- Fairfax County, Virginia, is applying the NCBC model in the after-school program of several middle schools in the county.
- Our Boston chapter is operating clubs to serve people who have psychiatric disabilities.
- Louisiana has a consortium of Families Helping Families with programs that provide a variety of social and educational services for individuals with ID and their families across the entire state. Many members of the consortium now serve as NCBC affiliates and operate book clubs.
- In St. Louis, the University of Missouri-St. Louis campus, the local Arc, and other community programs serving people with ID are collaborating to offer NCBC clubs.
- The Chicago NCBC has created a listserv and website and is conducting its own facilitator trainings.
- In Cincinnati, the county board of MR/DD is collaborating with the local public library; ten to twelve clubs are operating.
- In British Columbia, Canada, the Down Syndrome Research Foundation (DSRF) brought Tom Fish to Burnaby for initial training, and then sent two staff members to the NCBC Central Office in Columbus, Ohio, for further training and orientation. The two organizations have signed an agreement allowing the DSRF to train other agencies in Canada to become NCBC affiliates.

We believe it's everybody's responsibility to advocate inclusion and lifelong learning for people with disabilities. The NCBC is a first step, but it's only one event per week. We're looking at achieving a broader outcome—becoming an integral part of our members' social and vocational lives. Each club has a life and a culture of its own. We hope you find the approaches and activities in this book helpful but do not want to limit your collective creativity in running book clubs and promoting community inclusion. Our overall goal is lifelong learning, less isolation, and greater connection within local communities.

So we encourage you to use this book as a framework for operation and structure of your local NCBC program. But at the same time, please consider all the different ways that NCBC can be adapted to the specific needs, strengths, and cultures of your area and the wonderful people you are serving and supporting. Remember that boundaries only exist in our minds.

> **NCBC is . . .**
> - Lifelong learning
> - Less isolation
> - Greater connection

16 Frequently Asked Questions and Special Considerations

The following are answers and suggested solutions to some of the commonly asked questions and problems that people have encountered in running book clubs. We've organized them into the following categories:

- Club Operations
- Composition
- Group Dynamics
- Strategies

Club Operations

Q: *What are the **key factors** in running a sustained, **successful program**?*

A: 1. At least one affiliate organization or agency committed to supporting and maintaining the program.
2. Local program coordinators with good organizational and people skills who are enthusiastic about the program.
3. People with intellectual disabilities who have good family and community support, access to transportation, etc.
4. Sources for committed and enthusiastic volunteers, who may be parents, siblings, students, professionals, retirees, or people with disabilities.
5. Community sites to host book club meetings, such as bookstores, cafés, and coffee shops.

Q: *Do the book clubs have to **meet in a bookstore, café, or coffee shop**?*

A: More often than not, yes. Because each component of the NCBC model works to strengthen the others, it's vital that NCBC members have the opportunity to put their new literacy and social skills into practice out in the community. We consider exceptions on a case-by-case basis. (See Chapters 2 and 10 for specifics.)

The "sports club" reads the sports section of the newspaper and sports magazines together on Wednesdays.

Q: *What **books are in your library** and how do you select them?*

A: Our library consists of adapted (abridged) classic stories and popular fiction as well as newspapers and poetry. Reading material is chosen based on readability and popularity, and our library continues to grow as members request new stories. (See Appendix A.)

　　　There is a shortage of material written for adults that is at a reading level appropriate for many NCBC members. We rely most heavily on the adapted classic stories since they appeal to almost all readers.

Q: *What if members want to **keep their books**?*

A: If members would like to keep their books, they are welcome to buy them from the NCBC at a used-book price, depending on the age and condition of the book. We also recommend that they buy it from a used-book store or the bookstore where they meet, if they wish.

Q: *What about **members who join up after a club has already formed**? Are they encouraged to jump right in or to wait until a new book is begun? Do they buy their own books?*

A: We encourage new members to jump right in and current members to give them a summary of what's happening in the book. They receive a book from the program coordinator, unless all members of the club have purchased their books.

Q: *What is the **time commitment for the facilitators**?*

A: The time commitment for facilitators is approximately one and a half hours per week plus travel time. This includes arriving early to help set up tables, one hour for the meeting, and staying after to chat briefly with support staff or family. Facilitators are *not* expected to read the book ahead of time, as they would if they were participating as a member of a typical book club.

Q: *Should **facilitators come to meetings prepared** with activity ideas or supplies?*

A: This is helpful but not necessary. At their discretion, facilitators may bring ideas for activities from their training session and this book as well as materials related to the story. See Chapter 12 for detailed strategies and activity suggestions.

Q: *What does the **affiliate training** involve?*

A: We follow a "train-the-trainer model." This means local program coordinators have everything they need to recruit and train local volunteers and run the program. The Central Office trainer uses an interactive PowerPoint® presentation to explain the history of the NCBC program, the rationale behind our model, and details on how to plan and implement the program on a local level. We help the affiliate recruit volunteers and members for a demonstration book club that we conduct in a site of the affiliate's choosing. Then we open the floor to answer questions and help affiliates start working on their program plans.

Q: *What are the **costs involved with this program**?*

A: A detailed description of the fees for the affiliate training workshop is in Chapter 4. Costs to maintain the program are primarily to pay a part-time coordinator to administer the program. The only other costs are for supplies such as books, pens, markers, bookmarks, book bags, etc. We estimate these costs (other than administrative) to be about $200 per group, per year. For a detailed discussion of program costs and funding strategies, see "Program Funding" in Chapter 5 and "How To Approach Funding Sources and Community Organizations" in Chapter 13.

Composition

Q: *Should you **group members** according to **reading ability or age**?*

A: We have not seen the utility of intentionally grouping people in our Columbus clubs based on their reading ability, functional level, gender, age, or type of disability. We have taken all comers except those with disruptive or potentially aggressive behavior. We believe that diversity of members is a positive part of our clubs and often find that a range of reading abilities and ages enriches the club experience.

There are a few exceptions to this practice. Members of the Ohio Young Adult Transition Corps (YATC-Ohio), an AmeriCorps program housed in the OSU Nisonger Center, are serving as NCBC facilitators as part of their year of service. Due to the interests of specific YATC members, a new book club in Columbus draws its membership from the Ohio State School for the Blind. Other YATC members are recruiting people with physical disabilities to join a new book club that will support their common needs, though it is not exclusive.

Having said this, some NCBC coordinators in other communities have found that grouping works well for their clubs. We suggest you only consider grouping if you determine that the particular dynamics of your club dictate it.

Q: *What if you have* **more members for a group than you can handle** *and not enough volunteers to start another club?*

A: The program coordinator puts the prospective members' names on a waiting list and keeps them informed. Sometimes we offer a current member with good reading skills the opportunity to train as a Peer Activity Leader (PAL), which helps reduce the load for existing facilitators and may open up a slot for a new member. (See Chapter 6 for details.)

Group Dynamics

Q: *What if a* **group cannot agree on what book to read** *next?*

A: It's important to get input from members regarding the next book to read. However, we encourage our facilitators not to let this process become a power struggle. Ideally, the group can reach a consensus; if not, then they should vote. We ask facilitators to report their top three choices to the program coordinator. (See Chapter 12, Strategies and Activities That Encourage Social Interaction, item 49: "*Choose the Next Book.*")

Q: *What if some* **participants lose interest in a book** *after they've started it and others want to continue with it?*

A: We generally recommend sticking with a book to its conclusion. The reason is that it teaches members and facilitators to make the best of an imperfect situation. In some clubs, individual members have chosen to take a break from the club until the book they don't like is finished, then return for the next book. In other clubs, the entire group has voted to discontinue a book they found disappointing.

Q: *What if a* **member doesn't want to be there** *because someone else signed her up for the club without consulting her, she was unable to indicate whether or not she wanted to join, or some other reason?*

A: This situation occurs very rarely. We sometimes have members who start a club and then become bored or have scheduling conflicts and drop out of the club or change clubs. We also have members who drop out so they can participate in a seasonal activity and then return.

Q: *What if a* **member wants more of a relationship** *with a facilitator than the facilitator wants, or perhaps develops a crush on him or her and wants to change the emphasis from talking about books to other things?*

A: To avoid this type of situation, we encourage facilitators to set boundaries early on. One way to do this is to discuss members' rights and responsibilities and agree on a set of rules. These are discussed in Chapter 7. Members need to understand that NCBC is a weekly group activity; facilitators are volunteering their time, which is limited to about an hour a week except for when the club holds an event at the completion of a book.

Q: *What if one* **member tends to dominate the group,** *either by talking in lengthy monologues or otherwise stopping the free-flow of conversation and socialization among the other club members?*

A: Our training curriculum teaches facilitators to redirect the member back to the main topic, give her a specific task to do, or shorten the length of the activity. They can also use self-monitoring strategies such as poker chips or bingo markers to ensure that members have equal opportunities to speak.

Q: *What if a member does or says things that the other members find **extremely distracting, annoying, or frightening**?*

A: If a member is provocative, aggressive, or otherwise disruptive in a meeting, we suggest that the facilitator discuss this matter with the program coordinator. Then a specific plan of action should be put in place for the member to change her behavior. If no progress is noted after a reasonable amount of time, we suggest the coordinator explain the situation to a family member or support staff and ask the member to leave the club.

Q: *What if a **member of the group gets overly emotional** during a meeting?*

A: If a member becomes overly emotional, we suggest that a facilitator asks the member whether she wants to share her feelings with the group. If she is not willing or able to do so, one facilitator should take the member to a private area, try to calm her down, and find out the cause of her discomfort. If she is too distressed to rejoin the group, the facilitator should call her family or support staff and wait with the member until they arrive. Together they can make a decision about how to deal with her being upset. It may be best to ask her family or support staff to take her home.

Strategies

Q: *How can we best include **members who can't read**?*

A: The predominant technique used to include members who need more support in a book club is called "echo reading." It, and a variety of other strategies and activities for including emergent readers, is described in Chapter 12.

Q: *What if a **member wants more instruction in reading** than facilitators can give her in the course of a book club meeting?*

A: If members want reading instruction beyond what their book club can offer, facilitators might suggest that they attend more than one club (which several do) and set times throughout the week to read at home with family or support staff. The program coordinator may also refer members to local colleges or universities, library staff, or literacy organizations for individual or group tutoring.

Q: *What if one or two people in the group have **much stronger or weaker reading skills** than the other participants, so some members of the group are frustrated by too much or too little challenge in reading selections and activities?*

A: There is often considerable disparity between reading levels of members within the same club. We have always viewed this as a strength rather than a problem. Only rarely have any members left a club because they thought they were superior or inferior readers to other members. The clubs thrive on diversity. Our facilitators are trained to use specialized strategies with emergent readers and others with those with higher skills (see Chapter 12). Often, it is outsiders looking in who are more concerned about the reading disparity issue than the members or facilitators. To insiders, it's just part of the process that defines the NCBC.

Q: *What if others **can't understand a member's speech** when she reads aloud (and there are people in the group who cannot read the passage silently to themselves)?*

A: When a member's speech cannot be understood, we encourage one of the facilitators to repeat for them. In one of our groups, a parent serves this function for his daughter, who is extremely difficult to understand. Another member, whose voice is extremely difficult to hear, wears a portable microphone and speaker to augment her voice.

Q: *How can **people who cannot speak** participate?*

A: Some people who cannot speak or use sign language communicate with their own system of gestures or sounds. We encourage those members to have a family member or support staff sit in at meetings to help the group understand their communication. Various assistive technologies are available that allow text to be programmed in advance and spoken by devices. For more, see the Resources section of this book and the article in Appendix R, "Unique book club started for young adults" from *Western Springs Suburban Life*.

Appendix R (p. 195)

> *A speech therapist observed that one of her students, who is an NCBC member, all of a sudden is making leaps and bounds in his speech. (He is basically nonverbal, but is making more and more use of his 'voice.')*
>
> —Nann M, program coordinator and co-facilitator, Monroe, Louisiana

Q: *How can a member who uses an **augmentative communication device** participate?*

A: We encourage facilitators to work closely with family, support staff, and educators to develop and adapt approaches that consider the needs of everyone in the club. Family or support staff may need to program the augmentative device before the club meets to allow the member to take a turn reading. Members also can contribute their opinions on how to accommodate the member with communication challenges. When everyone works together, solutions that make sense for a specific book club usually emerge. The overall philosophy of NCBC is to keep things simple and realistic whenever possible. Various assistive technologies are available that allow text to be programmed in advance and spoken by devices. For more, see the Resources section of this book and the article in Appendix R, "Unique book club started for young adults" from *Western Springs Suburban Life*.

Q: *In general, how do you **accommodate people** with a range of disabilities?*

A: We want everyone to feel welcome in the book club, whatever his or her disability. The program coordinator (PC) will work with facilitators, the member, and her family or support staff to arrange whatever accommodations are possible.

Dan S (left) helps club members understand his stepdaughter Natalie's speech. Steven (right) is nonverbal and keys in his portion of the book each week for his DynaVox® to read aloud.

People who have difficulty speaking loudly and people with hearing impairments may benefit from adaptive listening devices that amplify sound with small microphones and speakers. See "Making Book Accommodations" in Chapter 5 for a discussion of accommodations for members with visual impairments. Additionally, our Resources section includes a list of useful websites, agencies, and organizations devoted to supporting people with disabilities.

We did have quite a time picking our second book, as one of the members is blind. I was stunned to find out that there are a great many books available in Braille—but very few in the reading level range that we are looking for. The group was great, however; the members just told me to find out what could be gotten and then tell them what they would be reading. One member stated that it would be pointless for them to get a book that not everyone could read.

The lead facilitator for Monday nights has also begun teaching a weekly sign language class. Two of her club members are severely hard of hearing. She read that learning sign language helps increase reading comprehension. Members of both book clubs she facilitates are attending as well as others who are not in the book club—they just want to be able to talk to their friends.

—Nann M, program coordinator and co-facilitator, Monroe, Louisiana

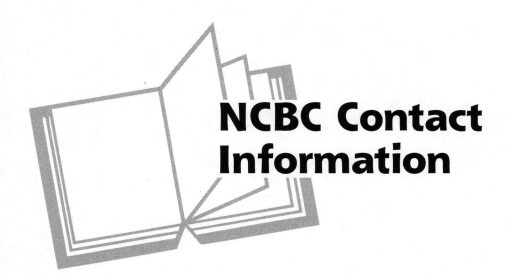

NCBC Contact Information

For any questions regarding this program, please contact the following persons:

Tom Fish, PhD, LISW
Next Chapter Book Club Program Director
(614) 292-7550
Fish.1@osu.edu

Paula Rabidoux, PhD/CCC
Next Chapter Book Club Language and Literacy Specialist
(614) 688-8472
Rabidoux.1@osu.edu

Jillian Ober, MA, CRC
Next Chapter Book Club Program Manager
(614) 247-6392
Ober.7@osu.edu

Vicki Graff, BA, BEd
Next Chapter Book Club Program Manager
(614) 688-8092
Graff.42@osu.edu

Glossary

Affiliate—A disability agency, advocacy group, family support group, or individual that the *program coordinator* is responsible to and often works for. The affiliate pays for and organizes the initial *NCBC* training and is responsible for ongoing overall operation of the program.

Community—A social group of people sharing an environment, often with shared interests.

Community Inclusion—Meaningful engagement in one's *community*; access to and involvement in common social pursuits (e.g., clubs, volunteerism); access to community resources and commerce.

Co-Facilitator—Refer to *Facilitator*.

Facilitator—A person, usually a volunteer, who is responsible for leading *Next Chapter Book Clubs*. The two or more facilitators who lead a club are called co-facilitators.

Host Site—A bookstore, café, or coffee shop where *Next Chapter Book Clubs* meet.

ID—The abbreviation for *Intellectual Disability*.

Inclusion—Refer to *Community Inclusion*.

Individualized Service Plan (ISP)—An individualized intervention plan for adults with disabilities. The ISP spells out all aspects of a person's wants and needs and then develops a plan of services and supports to address them.

Intellectual Disability (ID)—Refers to sub-average intellectual functioning that also involves deficits in adaptive behavior.

ISP—The abbreviation for *Individualized Service Plan*.

Literacy—A continuum of skills such as being able to read and write text; teaching and learning behaviors that will support and enhance literacy, which may include holding a book and turning pages, sliding a bookmark down a page, repeating words after someone, or making a comment about something that was read; all of the social behaviors that surround the "event" itself and how the person thinks and feels about literacy.

Member—An individual, usually with disabilities, who takes part in weekly sessions of *Next Chapter Book Clubs*.

NCBC—The abbreviation for *Next Chapter Book Club*.

Next Chapter Book Club (NCBC)—A program of The Ohio State University *Nisonger Center* committed to promoting *literacy* and social connection experiences for adolescents and adults with *intellectual disabilities* that encourage friendship and lifelong learning within a *community*-based setting.

Nisonger Center—An interdisciplinary program of The Ohio State University founded in 1966. The United States Administration on Developmental Disabilities has designated Nisonger Center as one of 67 "University Centers for Excellence in Developmental Disabilities" (UCEDDs). The mission of Nisonger Center is to work with communities to value and support the meaningful participation of people with disabilities of all ages through education, service, and research. The Center provides assistance to people with disabilities, families, service providers, and organizations to promote *inclusion* in education, health, employment, and *community* settings.

PAL—The abbreviation for *Peer Activity Leader*.

PC—The abbreviation for *Program Coordinator*.

Peer Activity Leader (PAL)—An *NCBC member* who is trained to volunteer as a *co-facilitator*. PALs take on a leadership role within their club, help others, and advance their own *literacy*, communication, and social skills.

Program Coordinator (PC)—The person responsible for overseeing all aspects of *NCBC* in his or her *community*. Responsibilities include training *facilitators*, recruiting *members* and facilitators, monitoring clubs, and identifying *host site* locations.

Self-Advocacy—The act of speaking up for one's rights, needs, and wants.

Self-Determination—The process of identifying and making choices that are important for oneself and then being responsible for those choices.

Social Connectedness—The extent to which an individual has friendships, engages in social activities, and feels a sense of belonging within his or her *community*.

Workshop, Sheltered—Employment site for persons with disabilities organized by government or private agencies.

Workshop, Training—A five- to six-hour workshop that the *NCBC* Central Office conducts to train staff and volunteers of new NCBC *affiliates* on how to operate the program.

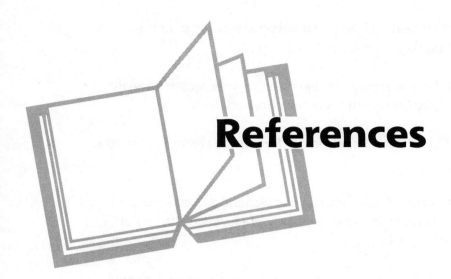

References

Abbeduto, L., and Hesketh, L.J. "Pragmatic development in individuals with mental retardation: learning to use language in social situations." *Mental Retardation and Developmental Disabilities Research Reviews*, 3, 1997: 323-333.

Bochner, S., Outhred, L., and Pieterse, M. A study of functional literacy skills in young adults with Down syndrome. *International Journal of Disability, Development and Education, 48,* 2001: 67-90.

Bramston, P., Bruggerman, K., and Pretty, G. Community perspectives and subjective quality of life. *International Journal of Disability, Development and Education, 49,* 2002: 385-397.

Bruner, J. The social context of language acquisition. *Language and Communication, 1,* 1981: 155-178.

Burns, M.S., Griffin, P., and Snow, C.E. *Starting out right: A guide to promoting children's reading success.* 1999; Washington, DC: National Academy Press.

Chadsey, J., and Beyer, S. Social relationships in the workplace. *Mental Retardation and Developmental Disabilities Research Reviews, 7,* 2001: 128-133.

Chipuer, H.M., Pretty, G.H., Delorey, E., Miller, M., Powers, T., Rumstein, O., Barnes, A., Cordasic, N., and Laurent, K. The Neighbourhood Youth Inventory: Development and validation. *Journal of Community and Applied Social Psychology, 9,* 1999: 355-368.

Cossu, G., and Marshall, J.C. Are cognitive skills a prerequisite for learning to read and write? *Cognitive Neuropsychology, 7,* 1990: 21-40.

Cossu, G., Rossini, F., and Marshall, J.C. When reading is acquired but phonemic awareness is not: A study of literacy in Down's syndrome. *Cognition, 46,* 1993: 129-138.

Fahrenthold, AL. Family volunteering and youth engagement in the non-profit sector: An analysis of benefits. 2003; Retrieved July 24, 2007, from http://www.serviceleader.org.

Fish, T., and Graff, V. Next Chapter Book Club: What A Novel Idea. *EP Exceptional Parent, 36 (11),* 2006: 46-48.

Fish, T.R., Graff, V.L.W., and Gross, A. Next Chapter Book Club: Lifelong learning and community inclusion. In W. L. Heward, *Exceptional children: An introduction to special education* (9th Ed.). 2009; Upper Saddle River, NJ: Merrill/Prentice Hall.

Fish, T.R., Rabidoux, P., Ober, J., and Graff, V.L. Community literacy and friendship model for people with intellectual disabilities. *Mental Retardation, 44 (6),* 2006: 443-446.

Fox, M. *Reading Magic.* 2001; San Diego: Harcourt, Inc.

Gracia, E., and Herrero, J. Determinants of social integration in the community: An exploratory analysis of personal, interpersonal and situational variables. *Journal of Community and Applied Social Psychology, 14,* 2004: 1-15.

Graham, C. Formal volunteering by the elderly: Trends, benefits, and implications for managers. 2003; Retrieved July 24, 2007, from http://www.serviceleader.org.

Grossman, J.B., and Furano, K. Making the most of volunteers. Public/Private Ventures Brief, Washington, DC. 2002; Quoted in Graham, 2003, retrieved July 24, 2007, from http://www.service-leader.org.

Guralnick, M.J. Peer interactions and the development of handicapped children's social and communicative competence. In H. Foot, M. Morgan, and R. Shute (Eds.), *Children helping children* (pp. 275–305). 1990; Sussex, England: John Wiley & Sons.

Guralnick, M.J., Connor, R.T., Neville, B., and Hammond, M.A. Promoting the peer-related social development of young children with mild developmental delays: Effectiveness of a comprehensive intervention. *American Journal on Mental Retardation, 111,* 2006: 336-356.

Henry, D., Keys, C., and Jopp, D. *The Community Living Attitudes Scales – Mental Retardation Version Reference Manual.* 1999; University of Illinois at Chicago Press.

Hunt, P., Haring, K., Farron-Davis, F., Staub, D., Beckstead, S., Curtis, D., Karasoff, P., and Sailor, W. Educational Practices in Integrated Settings Associated with Positive Student Outcomes. California: California Research Institute. 1992; Retrieved November 29, 2004, from ERIC database.

Kaderavek, J.N., and Rabidoux, P. Interactive to independent literacy: A model for designing literacy goals for children with atypical communication. *Reading and Writing Quarterly, 20 (3),* 2004: 237-260.

Kaderavek, J.N., and Sulzby, E. Issues in emergent literacy for children with specific language impairments: Language production during storybook reading, toy play and oral narratives. In L. R. Watson, T. L. Layton, E. R. Crais (Eds.), *Handbook of early language impairment in children: Volume II. Assessment and treatment* (pp. 199-244). 2000; New York: Delmar.

Katims, D.S. Literacy instruction for people with mental retardation: Historical highlights and contemporary analysis. *Education and Training in Mental Retardation and Developmental Disabilities, 35,* 2000: 3-15.

Kirchner, D.M. Reciprocal book reading: A discourse-based intervention strategy for the child with atypical language development. In T. M. Gallagher (Ed.), *Pragmatics of Language: Clinical Practices Issues* (pp. 307-332). 1991; San Diego: Singular.

Kliewer, C., and Landis, D. Individualizing literacy instruction for young children with moderate to severe disabilities. *Exceptional Children, 66,* 1999: 85-100.

Koppenhaver, D.A., Coleman, P.P., Kalman, S.L., and Yoder, D.E. The implications of emergent literacy research for children with developmental disabilities. *American Journal of Speech-Language Pathology: A Journal of Clinical Practice, 1,* 1991: 38-44.

Kruidenier, J. *Research-Based Principles for Adult Basic Education Reading Instruction.* The Partnership for Reading. 2002; Jessup, Md.: The National Institute for Literacy.

Layton, L., and Miller, C. Interpretations of literacy. *Cambridge Journal of Education, 34,* 2004: 51-63.

Lunsky, Y., and Neely, L. Extra-individual sources of social support as described by adults with mild intellectual disabilities. *Mental Retardation, 40 (4),* 2002: 269-77.

Minnes, P., Buell, K., Feldman, M., McColl, M.A., and McCreary, B. Community integration as acculturation: Preliminary validation of the AIMS interview. *Journal of Applied Research in Intellectual Disabilities, 15,* 2002: 377-387.

Moni, K.B., and Jobling, A. Reading-related literacy learning of young adults with Down syndrome: Findings from a three year teaching and research program. *International Journal of Disability, Development and Education, 48,* 2001: 377-394.

National Adult Literacy Survey: 2002; Retrieved December 9, 2004, from http://www.nifl.gov/.

National Institute for Literacy. *Disability and literacy: How disability issues are addressed in adult basic education programs.* 1997; Office of Adult and Vocational Education, U.S. Department of Education.

National Reading Panel. Report of the national reading panel: Teaching Children to Read. 2000; Washington, DC: National Institute of Child Health and Human Development.

National Reading Panel. Report of the national reading panel: Teaching Children to Read - Reports of the Subgroups. 2000; Washington, DC: National Institute of Child Health and Human Development.

Nisbet, J., and Hagner, D. *Part of the community: Strategies for including everyone.* 2000; Baltimore, Md.: Paul H. Brookes Publishing Co.

Novak Amado, A. *Friendships and community connections between people with and without intellectual disabilities.* 1993; Baltimore, Md.: Paul H. Brookes Publishing Co., Inc.

O'Brien, J., and O'Brien, C. Unlikely alliances: Friendships and people with developmental disabilities. *Perspectives on Community Building.* Georgia: Responsive Systems Associates. 1993; Retrieved November 29, 2004, from ERIC database.

Ochs, E., and Schieffelin, B.B. *Acquiring conversational competency.* 1983; London: Routledge and Kegan Paul.

Ochs, E., Taylor, C., Rudolph, D., and Smith, R. Storytelling as a theory-building activity. *Discourse Processes, 15,* 1992: 37-72.

Ohio Rehabilitation Services Commission (RSC) *Federal Fiscal Year 2002 Vocational Rehabilitation Annual Program Report.* 2003; Columbus: Ohio Rehabilitation Services Commission.

Post, S., and Neimark, J. *Why Good Things Happen to Good People.* 2007; Broadway Books. Retrieved July 23, 2007, from http://www.whygoodthingshappen.com.

Pottie, C., and Sumarah, J. Friendships between persons with and without developmental disabilities. *Mental Retardation, 42 (1),* 2004: 55-66.

Ratner, N.B., Parker, B., and Gardner, P. Joint book reading as a language scaffolding activity for communicatively impaired children. *Seminars in Speech and Language, 14,* 1993: 296-313.

Renzaglia, A., Karvonen, M., Drasgow, E., and Stoxen, C. Promoting a lifetime of inclusion. *Focus on Autism and Other Developmental Disabilities, 18,* 2003. Retrieved November 29, 2004, from ERIC database.

Schieffelin, B.B., and Cochran-Smith, M. Learning to read culturally: Literacy before schooling. In H. Goelman, A. Oberg, and F. Smith (Eds.). *Awakening to literacy* (pp. 3-23). 1984; London: Heinemann.

Scollon, R., and Scollon, S.B.K. *Narrative, literacy, and face in interethnic communication.* 1981; Norwood, NJ: Ablex Publishing.

Seigel, J. The Ethnograph v 5.0. 1998; Thousand Oaks, CA: Scolari Sage Publications.

Smith, P. Drawing new maps: A radical cartography of developmental disabilities. *Review of Educational Research, 69,* 1999: 117-144.

Snow, C., and Ninio, A. The contracts of literacy: What children learn from learning to read books. In W. H. Teale and E. Sulzby (Eds.), *Emergent literacy: Writing and reading* (pp. 116-138). 1986; Norwood, NJ: Ablex Publishing.

Teale, W.H., and Sulzby, E. Emergent literacy as a perspective for examining how young children become readers and writers. In W. H. Teale and E. Sulzby (Eds.), *Emergent literacy: Writing and reading* (pp. vii-xxv). 1986; Norwood, N.J.: Ablex Publishing.

U.S. Equal Employment Opportunity Commission. Questions and answers about persons with intellectual disabilities in the workplace and the Americans with Disabilities Act. Retrieved December 6, 2004, from http://www.eeoc.gov/facts/intellectual_disabilities.html.

Vacca, J., Vacca, R.T., and Gove, M. *Reading and learning to read* (3rd Ed.). 1995; New York: HarperCollins College Publishers.

Wagner, M., Newman, L., Cameto, R., Garza, N., and Levine, P. National Longitudinal Transition Study 2; Life after high school for youth with disabilities. 2004; Prepared for Office of Special Education Programs, U.S. Dept. of Education, SRI International.

Wagner, M., Newman, L., Cameto, R., Garza, N., and Levine, P. *After high school: A first look at the post-school experiences of youth with disabilities. A report from the National Longitudinal Transition Study-2 (NLTS2).* 2005; Menlo Park, CA: SRI International.

Wagner, M., Newman, L., Cameto, R., and Levine, P. *Changes over time in the early postschool outcomes of youth with disabilities. A report of findings from the National Longitudinal Transition Study (NLTS) and the National Longitudinal Transition Study-2 (NLTS2).* 2005; Menlo Park, CA: SRI International.

Watson, L.R., Layton, T.L., Pierce, P.L., and Abraham, L.M. Enhancing emerging literacy in a language preschool. *Language, Speech, and Hearing Services in Schools, 25,* 1994: 136-145.

Wehmeyer, M.L. and Schwartz, M. Self-determination and positive adult outcomes: A follow-up study of youth with mental retardation and learning disabilities. *Exceptional Children, 63,* 1998: 245-255.

Wilson, J. Volunteering. *Annual Review of Sociology, 26,* 2000: 215-240. Quoted in Graham, 2003, retrieved July 24, 2007, from http://www.serviceleader.org.

Yates, M., and Youniss, J. *Roots of Civic Identity: International Perspectives on Community Services and Activism in Youth.* 1999; Cambridge University Press: Cambridge. Cited in Fahrenthold, 2003, retrieved July 24, 2007, from http://www.serviceleader.org.

Young and Glasgow. Volunteering and healthy aging: What we know. http://www.volunteer.ca. 1998; Quoted in Graham, 2003, retrieved July 24, 2007, from http://www.serviceleader.org.

Resources

Augmentative Communication Technology Supports

A website offering augmentative and alternative communication (AAC) resources for people with severe speech impairments.

5225 Old Orchard Road

Suite 46

Skokie, IL 60077

Phone: 847-966-8963

Email: jsenner@actsil.org

Website: http://www.actsil.org

Center for Self-Determination

This website discusses the importance of personal control over one's life.

Website: http://www.self-determination.com

The Centre for Literacy [Le centre d'alphabétisation]

The Centre for Literacy of Quebec is a Montreal-based resource, professional development, and research centre that supports best practices and informed policy development in literacy, by creating bridges between research, policy, and practice. The Centre looks toward a society where lifelong learning opportunities and community supports enable all individuals to participate fully in their communities as family members, citizens, and workers.

3040 Sherbrooke Street West

Room 4B.5A

Montreal, Quebec, Canada H3Z 1A4

Phone: 514-931-8731, local 1415

Website: http://www.centreforliteracy.qc.ca/

Don Johnston, Inc.

Don Johnston, Inc. develops industry-standard interventions addressing every area of literacy—word study, reading, and writing—as well as supports learning in content areas.

26799 W. Commerce Drive

Volo, IL 60073

Phone: 800-999-4660

Website: http://www.donjohnston.com/about/epfrm.htm

DynaVox Technologies

This company provides augmentative and alternative communication (AAC) products to help individuals and families who need alternatives to gain, or regain, the power of speech.

2100 Wharton Street

Suite 400

Pittsburgh, PA 15203

Phone: 1-866-DYNAVOX or 412-381-4883

Fax: 412-381-5241

Website: http://www.dynavoxtech.com

Exceptional Parent Magazine

This monthly magazine was established in 1971 as "the Family and Professional Journal for the Special Needs Community." Feature articles cover issues relating to infants, children, adolescents, and adults with physical, mental, and intellectual disabilities, and their families. The website has a Resources section with many helpful links to products, services, blogs, and other organizations.

416 Main Street

Johnstown, PA 15901

Phone: 877-372-7368

Email: EPAR@kable.com

Website: http://www.eparent.com

Institute for Community Inclusion (ICI)

ICI promotes inclusion for people with disabilities. Their services focus on the entire life span of people with all types of disabilities.

Institute for Community Inclusion/UCEDD

UMass Boston

100 Morrissey Blvd.

Boston, MA 02125

Phone: 617-287-4300

Fax: 617-287-4352

TTY: 617-287-4350

Email: ici@umb.edu

Website: http://www.communityinclusion.org

Listen Technologies Corp.

Listen Technologies Corp. is a source for FM listening devices, microphones, speakers, and other audio equipment for people with hearing impairments.

> 14912 Heritagecrest Way
> Bluffdale, UT 84065-4818
> Phone: 801-233-8992
> Website: http://www.listentech.com

LiteracyCenter.Net—Early Childhood Education Network

LiteracyCenter.Net provides high-quality, research-based, education materials each day to children worldwide. Online lessons are free of advertising and free of charge.

> Literacy Center Education Network
> 131 Vista Robles
> Ben Lomond, CA 95005
> Website: http://www.literacycenter.net

National Institute for Literacy's Adult Education Reading Instruction

This website presents evidenced-based practices for teaching reading to adults in adult basic education and family literacy programs. The suggestions for basic reading instruction with adults that are presented are the result of an evaluation of the research conducted by the Reading Research Working Group (RRWG), a collaborative effort of the National Institute for Literacy and the National Center for the Study of Adult Learning and Literacy.

> National Institute for Literacy
> National Institute of Child Health and Human Development
> US Department of Education
> US Department of Health and Human Services
> 1775 I Street NW, Suite 730
> Washington, DC 20006
> Phone: 202-233-2025
> Fax: 202-233-2050
> Websites: http://www.nifl.gov/partnershipforreading/adult_reading/adult_reading.html;
> http://www.nifl.gov/partnershipforreading/adult_reading/alphabetics/alphaassess5.html

National Library Service for the Blind and Physically Handicapped (NLS)
(The Library of Congress)

Through a national network of cooperating libraries, the NLS administers a free library program of Braille and audio materials circulated to eligible borrowers in the United States by postage-free mail. The NLS publishes *Talking Book Topics*, a bimonthly list of recent audio books; *Braille Book Review*, a bimonthly list of recent Braille books; and annual catalogs of recorded and Braille books and magazines.

> 1291 Taylor Street, NW
> Washington, DC 20011
> Phone: 202-707-5100; 1-888-NLS-READ
> TDD: 202-707-0744
> Fax: 202-707-0712
> Website: http://www.loc.gov/nls

News for You®

A weekly newspaper for adult learners published weekly by New Readers Press. The four-page newspaper features stories based on articles from the Associated Press and the Los Angeles Times-Washington Post News Service, rewritten for adults with lower reading skills. It covers a wide variety of topics and uses colorful photos and graphics. The classroom package with ten copies also includes a Teacher's Guide with vocabulary, tips before reading the stories, and discussion questions.

New Readers Press
1320 Jamesville Avenue
Syracuse, NY 13210
Phone: 315-422-9121
Toll free: 800-448-8878
Toll free fax: 866-894-2100
Email: nrp@proliteracy.org
Websites: http://www.news-for-you.com; http://www.newreaderspress.com

The Ohio State University Nisonger Center

The home of the Next Chapter Book Club, the Nisonger Center is one of sixty-seven "University Centers for Excellence in Developmental Disabilities." The mission of Nisonger Center is to work with communities to value and support the meaningful participation of people with disabilities of all ages through education, service, and research. The Center provides assistance to people with disabilities, families, service providers, and organizations to promote inclusion in education, health, employment, and community settings.

357 McCampbell Hall
1581 Dodd Drive
Columbus, OH 43210
Phone: 614-292-0775
Fax: 614-292-3727
Email: meck.1@osu.edu
Website: http://nisonger.osu.edu

Social Skill Builder, Inc.

This company presents a series of interactive software programs that provide valuable social training (targeting emotions, behaviors, and interactions) through video scenarios and motivating technology.

PO Box 2430
Leesburg, VA 20177
Phone: 1-866-278-1452
Fax: 703-669-1258
Email: info@socialskillbuilder.com
Website: http://www.socialskillbuilder.com

Stevenson Reading Program
Published by Stevenson Learning Skills, Inc., The Stevenson Reading Program is an alternative approach for teaching reading, spelling, and other basic language skills to typical students as well as those with learning difficulties.

> 451 Elm Street, Unit 2
> North Attleboro, MA 02760-3313
> Phone: 800-343-1211
> Fax: 508-699-4279
> Email: info@stevensonlearning.com
> Website: http://www.stevensonlearning.com

Telex Communications
Telex Professor is a digital and tape talking book player that also includes an accessible radio.

> 12000 Portland Ave. S
> Burnsville, MN 55337
> Phone: 952-887-7406 or 952-887-5546
> Website: http://www.telex.com/talkingbook

Time Warner Cable's Time to Read
This tutoring and mentoring program trains volunteers to use innovative teaching methods and materials with people who want to improve their reading. Time to Read augments existing education and literacy programs and helps adolescents succeed and stay in school. For adults, it provides the bridge between basic literacy programs and high school equivalency programs. The website includes links to a wealth of online literacy resources.

> 290 Harbor Drive
> Stamford, CT 06902
> Phone: 212-522-3927
> Email: timetoread@twcable.com
> Website: http://www.timetoread.com

United Nations Volunteers
The United Nations Volunteers (UNV) program is the UN organization that contributes to peace and development through volunteerism worldwide. This website discusses the benefits and importance of volunteerism.

> Postfach 260 111
> D-53153 Bonn, Germany
> Phone: +49-228-815 2000
> Fax: +49-228-815 2001
> Email: information@unvolunteers.org
> Website: http://www.unv.org

External Downloadable Resources

Carl's Corner Website
This website provides free and printable literacy activities.
> Email: carl1404@msn.com
> Website: http://carlscorner.us.com

"Sight" and High Frequency Words Website
This website provides lists of "sight" and high-frequency words that can be used for literacy activities. Consider using these in conjunction with the resources provided by Carl's Corner Website and others. Write the words on index cards, add dice and place keepers, and you have made a word game.
> Website: http://www.usu.edu/teachall/text/reading/highfrequency.htm

TeAch-nology Bingo Cards
From this website you can make word bingo sheets. Use some of the words from the high-frequency word website and enter them into the word bingo site. Hit the scramble button to create various bingo cards, print them off, and laminate them. Then use pennies or other objects as place markers. You can also make sentences of the words as you call them out one at a time.
> Teachnology, Incorporated
> 87 Grandview Drive
> Bloomingburg, NY 12721
> Website: http://www.teach-nology.com/web_tools/materials/bingo

The board games and the bingo are only a few of the possibilities. You can also create word sorting cards from the word sorts lists on the first site, Carl's Corner. Use both words and pictures. The objective is to sort the words in some fashion like beginning consonants, rhymes, endings, number of syllables, long or short vowel sounds, or concepts.

Suggested Reading

Fox, M. *Reading Magic.* 2001; San Diego: Harcourt, Inc.
> This book teaches parents of children ages zero to seven "how your child can learn to read before school and other read aloud miracles." Mem Fox is the author of twenty-nine books for children and formerly Associate Professor of Literacy Studies in the School of Education at Flinders University, South Australia. Before retiring in 1996, Fox taught there for twenty-four years. She travels worldwide as an international literacy consultant urging parents, teachers, and others to read aloud to children.
> Website: http://www.memfox.net

National Institute for Literacy. *Disability and literacy: How disability issues are addressed in adult basic education programs.* 1997; Office of Adult and Vocational Education, U.S. Department of Education.
> This article discusses recent findings regarding literacy and the disability community.
> Website: http://www.nifl.gov/nifl/ld/archive/disabliter.htm

Voss, K. *Teaching by Design: Using Your Computer to Create Materials for Students with Learning Differences.*
Authored by Kimberly Voss and published by Woodbine House, this book includes step-by-step instruction for designing thirty types of educational materials for children and adults with a wide range of special needs. Suitable for designing literacy activities, the included CD-ROM provides templates for lotto boards, matching games, sentences strips, and more.
Website: http://www.woodbinehouse.com

Appendices

A: Next Chapter Book Club Library / 163

B: Member Intake Form / 165

C: Facilitator Intake Form / 166

D: Facilitator Position Description / 167

E: Monthly Facilitator Report / 168

F: Member End-of-Book Survey / 171

G: Certificate of Accomplishment / 172

H: Five-Level Scale of Literacy Skills / 173

I: ECO-NCBC Literacy Observations / 174

J: Family/Staff Expectations Survey / 175

K: Family/Staff Satisfaction Survey / 177

L: Questions for Member Interviews / 180

M: Chuckie's Questionnaire / 182

N: Questions for Facilitator Interviews / 184

O: Community Inclusion Survey for Members BEFORE Book Club / 186

P: Community Inclusion-Location Survey for Members
    AFTER Book Club / 189

Q: Community Living Attitudes Scale (Adapted) / 193

R: *Western Springs Suburban Life* article: "Unique book club started
    for young adults" / 195

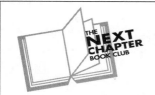

Next Chapter Book Club
Library

Adapted Classics

A Christmas Carol

A Little Princess

A Wind in the Door

A Wrinkle in Time

Alice's Adventures in Wonderland

Anne of Green Gables

Anne Of Green Gables—
   Christmas Stories

Around the World in 80 Days

Black Beauty

Charlotte's Web

Gulliver's Travels

Heidi

Little House on the Prairie series

Little Women

Moby Dick

Oliver Twist

Peter Pan

Pinocchio

Pollyanna

Rebecca of Sunnybrook Farm

Robinson Crusoe

Stuart Little

The Adventures of Huckleberry Finn

The Adventures of Robin Hood

The Adventures of Sherlock Holmes

The Adventures of Tom Sawyer

The Call of the Wild

The Legend of Sleepy Hollow

The Lion, the Witch, and the
   Wardrobe

The Secret Garden

The Story of Dr. Dolittle

The Story of King Arthur and His
   Knights

The Strange Case of Dr. Jekyll and
   Mr. Hyde

The Swiss Family Robinson

The Three Musketeers

The Time Machine

The Trumpet of the Swan

The Wind in the Willows

The Wonderful Wizard of Oz

Through the Looking Glass

Treasure Island

White Fang

Popular Fiction

Al Capone Does My Shirts
Because of Winn-Dixie
Blubber
Buffalo Bill and the Pony Express
Caddie Woodlawn
Flicka: A Friend for Katy
Freckle Juice
Harry Potter and the Sorcerer's Stone (Book 1)
Harry Potter and the Chamber of Secrets (Book 2)
Harry Potter and the Prisoner of Azkaban (Book 3)
Hatchet
Henry and Ribsy
Henry Huggins
Hoops
Joey Pigza Swallowed the Key

Knights of the Kitchen Table
My Side of the Mountain
Ramona and Her Father
Ramona Quimby, Age 8
Runaway Ralph
Skinny Bones
Stealing Freedom
The Boxcar Children
The Enormous Egg
The Green Mile
The Mouse and the Motorcycle
The Riding Club Crime (Nancy Drew)
The River
The True Confessions of Charlotte Doyle
Where the Red Fern Grows

Miscellaneous

Chicken Soup for the Soul (non-fiction)
Count Us In: Growing Up With Down Syndrome (advocacy)
"News for You" (adapted newspaper)
Sports page of the newspaper
Where the Sidewalk Ends (poetry)

Next Chapter Book Club
Member Intake Form

1. What is your name? _____

2. How old are you? _____Birthdate?_____

3. What is your phone number? _____

4. What is your address? _____

    _____

5. Do you live alone? Do you live with family or roommates?

    _____

6. What days and times are you available to participate in the NCBC?

    _____

7. What kind of books would you like to read?

    _____

8. Are there things you shouldn't eat or drink? Do you have any health concerns (ex. seizures) or special needs we should know about?

    _____

9. Who should we contact in case of an emergency? Phone number?

    _____

10. Who told you about the Next Chapter Book Club?

    _____

Please read or listen carefully to the following statements.

I understand the Next Chapter Book Club (NCBC) staff may take and use my photograph for the purpose of advertising the program. I also understand the NCBC will be unable to include me in a book club if my behavior is disruptive or aggressive because it can disturb other members of the club. I understand the NCBC has the right to ask me to leave the group if my behavior is disruptive or otherwise inappropriate.

_____   _____
Name   Date

_____   _____
(Guardian, if appropriate)   Date

© 2007-2009 Next Chapter Book Club

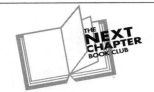

Next Chapter Book Club
Facilitator Intake Form

1. Name: _____

2. Phone number: _____

3. Address: _____

4. Email: _____

5. Occupation: _____

6. How would you describe yourself? _____

7. Have you been involved with individuals with MR/DD in the past? YES   NO

   If yes, how? _____

8. What experience have you had with volunteer work? _____

9. How did you hear about the NCBC? _____

10. What concerns, if any, do you have about facilitating a book club?

    _____

11. When would you like to begin facilitating a book club? _____

12. What days and/or evenings and times are you available to facilitate?

    _____

13. Have you ever been convicted of a felony? If yes, please explain.

    _____

14. Are you an insured driver? _____

Please read the following statements carefully and sign below.

I will protect the privacy of all participants in my book club and keep all information shared by and about the participants confidential.

I understand the Next Chapter Book Club (NCBC) staff may take and use my photograph for the purpose of publicizing the program.

I certify that the information provided above is true to the best of my knowledge.

_____   _____
Volunteer Facilitator   Date

© 2007-2009 Next Chapter Book Club

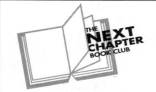

Next Chapter Book Club
Facilitator Position Description

Title: Volunteer Facilitator

Location of service (community setting)**:**

Length of service: One to two hours, each week, until at least one book is finished (approx. 3 months)

Report to (Program Coordinator's name, email address, and phone number)**:**

Position Summary:
With support from Next Chapter Book Club (NCBC) staff, volunteer facilitators guide activities in weekly, community-based book clubs for adolescents and adults with intellectual disabilities. The primary function of this position is to promote literacy learning, social connectedness, and community inclusion for book club members. Working in teams of two, volunteer facilitators also communicate regularly with NCBC staff and perform group management tasks such as monitoring and encouraging attendance.

Qualifications:
- Desire and commitment to work with adolescents and adults with intellectual disabilities (previous experience is not necessary, but may be helpful)
- Ability to travel to weekly book club meetings
- Enthusiasm, creativity, and good "people skills" are essential

Position Responsibilities:
- Use activities and strategies learned in training to promote literacy learning, social connectedness, and community inclusion during book club
- Develop working relationship with co-facilitator and negotiate group tasks
- Contact each member prior to each meeting to remind them of book club
- Monitor member attendance; notify NCBC staff of any extended member absence
- Complete monthly facilitator reports and maintain communication with NCBC staff (i.e., respond to emails or phone calls)
- Promptly attend weekly, one-hour book club meetings at designated community location for the length of at least one book (approx. 3 months)
- Inform co-facilitator and NCBC staff in advance (if possible) of any absence
- Notify NCBC staff two weeks in advance (if possible) of needing a new book; lead members in a vote for the new book
- <u>Respect the talent, abilities, and privacy of all book club members</u>

Compliance requirement:
- Background check through _____ (your state's) Bureau of Criminal Investigation

I have read and understand the above NCBC volunteer facilitator position description.

_____   _____
Facilitator Signature   Date

Next Chapter Book Club
Monthly Facilitator Report

Section One: Meeting Information

Name: _____

Report Date: _____

Book Club Time/Location: _____

Meeting 1 Members Present:	Date: Members Absent:	(MM/DD/YYYY)
Meeting 2 Members Present:	Date: Members Absent:	(MM/DD/YYYY)
Meeting 3 Members Present:	Date: Members Absent:	(MM/DD/YYYY)
Meeting 4 Members Present:	Date: Members Absent:	(MM/DD/YYYY)

1. Did absent members notify you ahead of time?

    Yes   No   If yes, how? _____

2. What is the primary reason for the absences?

    Illness   Lack of transportation   Other commitment   Forgot   Other

3. Were there any efforts made to improve attendance?

    Describe _____

    _____

© 2007-2009 Next Chapter Book Club

NCBC Monthly Facilitator Report   Page 2

Section Two: Literacy and Social Connectedness

Literacy

1. Approximately how many pages do you read each week? (in multiples of 5)

2. Has your group participated in literacy activities other than reading?   Yes   No

    If so, what kind?_____

    _____

3. I have observed improvement in reading, writing, or other literacy skills:

    Consistently   Often   Occasionally   Seldom   Never

4. I have observed improvements in literacy skills in:

    One specific member   A specific subgroup   The entire group

    Different members each week   No members

Social Connectedness

1. I have observed indicators (ex. more member-to-member conversations) of increased
    social connectedness:

    Consistently   Often   Occasionally   Seldom   Never

    Describe _____

    _____

2. I have observed indicators of increased social connectedness in:

    One specific member   A specific subgroup   The entire group

    Different members each week   No members

    Describe _____

    _____

3. How do you promote friendships in your book club?_____

    _____

    _____

Section Three: Community Inclusion and General Questions

Community Inclusion

1. Describe any significant member interaction with host site staff or customers.

   _____

   _____

2. Describe any noticeable reactions (positive or negative) from host site staff or customers to the presence of the book club. _____

   _____

   _____

3. How comfortable do your members appear to be in the community setting? Do they order their own refreshments?_____

   _____

   _____

General Questions

1. Are there any emerging issues that need to be addressed in your group? Is your group ready to start a new book?_____

   _____

   _____

2. What is your motivation for coming to book club each week?

   _____

   _____

3. Do you have any thoughts, feelings, or ideas you would like to share? What would you change about the NCBC?_____

   _____

   _____

Glossary

Literacy – Being able to read and write text; teaching and learning behaviors that will support and enhance literacy, which may include holding a book and turning pages, sliding a bookmark down a page, repeating words after someone or making a comment about something that was read; all of the social behaviors that surround the "event" itself and how the person thinks and feels about literacy.

Social Connectedness – The extent to which an individual has friendships, engages in social activity, and feels a sense of belonging.

Community Inclusion – Meaningful engagement in one's community; access to and involvement in common social pursuits (i.e., clubs, volunteerism); access to community resources and commerce.

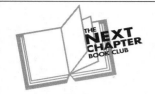

Appendix F

Next Chapter Book Club
Member End-of-Book Survey

Name: _____ Date: _____

Group facilitators: _____

What book did you read? _____

Did you enjoy the book?   YES   NO   SORT OF   What did you like about it?

_____

What did you learn from reading this book? _____

_____

Do you enjoy being in the NCBC?   YES   NO   SOMETIMES

What do like most about being in the NCBC? _____

What do you like the least about being in the NCBC? _____

Do you feel your reading abilities have improved from being a part of
the book club?
_____

Have you made any new friends? If yes, what are their names?

_____

What do you think about meeting in the café/bookstore/coffee shop?

_____

Do you tell your friends about your book club? If yes, what do you tell them?

_____

Do you want to continue to participate in the NCBC? Why or why not?

_____

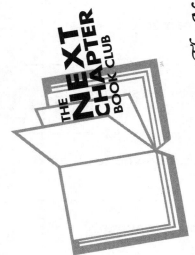

The Next Chapter Book Club awards this

Certificate of Accomplishment

To

_____

in recognition of your successful completion of

_____

this _____ day of _____, in the year _____.

Signed _____

© 2007-2009 Next Chapter Book Club

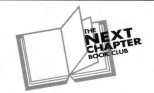

Next Chapter Book Club
Five-Level Scale of Literacy Skills

Member Name: _____

Date: _____

Observer: _____

Choose the member's reading level you have observed during NCBC meetings.

Reading Level

_____ Level I – no letter recognition or understanding of written language

_____ Level II – recognizes and understands letters

_____ Level III – reads and understands single words

_____ Level IV – reads and understands sentences

_____ Level V – reads and understands paragraphs

Next Chapter Book Club
ECO-NCBC Literacy Observations

Member Name: _____

Date: _____

Observer: _____

Describe how often you observed the events below during the NCBC meeting. Circle the number that applies.   1 = Never   2 = Seldom
3 = Occasionally   4 = Often   5 = Consistently   NA = not applicable

Social Exchange

1.	Enjoys reading with others.	1....2....3....4....5....NA
2.	"Reads" alone.	1....2....3....4....5....NA
3.	Pays attention to both book and participants.	1....2....3....4....5....NA
4.	Takes turns with participants.	1....2....3....4....5....NA
5.	Cooperates with participants.	1....2....3....4....5....NA

Language

1.	Imitates participants' words.	1....2....3....4....5....NA
2.	Responds when participants comment.	1....2....3....4....5....NA
3.	Answers questions verbally.	1....2....3....4....5....NA
4.	Communicates verbally.	1....2....3....4....5....NA
5.	Talks to participants for the fun of it.	1....2....3....4....5....NA
6.	Talks to request or control.	1....2....3....4....5....NA
7.	Talks to self.	1....2....3....4....5....NA

Conversation

1.	Talks about a variety of topics.	1....2....3....4....5....NA
2.	Stays communicating on a topic.	1....2....3....4....5....NA
3.	Talks inappropriately or off-topic.	1....2....3....4....5....NA

Literacy

1.	Attempts to turn pages of book.	1....2....3....4....5....NA
2.	Points to pictures.	1....2....3....4....5....NA
3.	Points to print.	1....2....3....4....5....NA
4.	Comments on connections between book and life.	1....2....3....4....5....NA
5.	Predicts story events. (What happens next?)	1....2....3....4....5....NA
6.	Reads letters.	1....2....3....4....5....NA
7.	Reads words.	1....2....3....4....5....NA
8.	Labels illustrations.	1....2....3....4....5....NA
9.	Initiates familiar, repetitive phrases from story.	1....2....3....4....5....NA
10.	Initiates comments about story.	1....2....3....4....5....NA
11.	Extends conversation from story.	1....2....3....4....5....NA

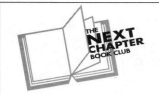

Appendix J

Next Chapter Book Club
Family/Staff Expectations Survey

Date of Interview: _____

NCBC Member Information

NCBC member name: _____

Age of NCBC member: _____

Name of person being interviewed (interviewee): _____

_____

Interviewee's relationship to NCBC member: _____

Interviewee's age: _____

Where does the NCBC member live? _____

Education of NCBC member (functional academics): _____

What (if any) additional classes has the member participated in (tutoring, adult

education)? _____

NCBC member's current work: _____

---

1. How did <u>you</u> hear about the NCBC? _____

   _____

2. What is the main reason you were interested in having your family member
   (or consumer) join the NCBC? _____

   _____

3. What hopes and expectations do you have for your family member's
   participation in the NCBC? _____

   _____

NCBC Family/Staff Expectations Survey   Page 2

4.   These days, how often and what does your family member/consumer read?

_____

5.   On a scale from 1 to 5, where 1 is not at all satisfied and 5 is completely
      satisfied, how satisfied is your family member with his/her social life?

              1   2   3   4   5

6.   Again, on a scale from 1 to 5, how satisfied is your family member with his/her
      degree of community participation?

              1   2   3   4   5

7.   On a scale from 1 to 5, where 1 is no enjoyment and 5 is much enjoyment,
      how much enjoyment does your family member derive from reading?

              1   2   3   4   5

8.   On a scale from 1 to 5, where 1 is not interested and 5 is always interested,
      how much interest does your family member show in reading?

              1   2   3   4   5

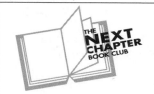

Appendix K

Next Chapter Book Club
Family/Staff Satisfaction Survey

Date of Interview: _____

NCBC Member Information

NCBC member name: _____

Age of NCBC member: _____

Name of person being interviewed (interviewee): _____

_____

Interviewee's relationship to NCBC member: _____

Interviewee's age: _____

How long has the member been involved with a NCBC book club? _____

Where does the NCBC member live? _____

What (if any) additional classes or clubs has the member joined since starting the

NCBC (tutoring, adult education)? _____

NCBC member's current work: _____

---

1. What were your hopes and expectations for your family member's participation in the NCBC?_____

   _____

2. What are one or two things your family member or consumer likes about the book club? _____

   _____

3. Has his/her reading changed since beginning the book club? (Does s/he read more independently, at a higher level?) _____

   _____

NCBC Family/Staff Satisfaction Survey   Page 2

4. Has his/her interest and comfort level with being in social settings changed since s/he has been in the NCBC? Please give an example:

    _____

    _____

5. Have you noticed any changes in his/her social interactions?

        Does s/he talk about his/her friends?

        Is s/he socializing with people in the book club?

        Is s/he more confident in his/her social relationships?

        Have his/her problem solving skills changed?

        Have his/her social behaviors become more appropriate?

        Does s/he ever mention the NCBC in conversations with others?

6. Does s/he perceive changes in his/her social life (such as more friends or greater acceptance)?

    _____

    _____

7. Do you feel your family member or consumer is more assertive since starting the book club (states his/her opinion more readily, disagrees with people, or asks questions of others)?

    _____

    _____

8. Have you noticed any changes in your family member's/consumer's general behavior at home or work (more attentive, more productive or on task at work, more confident)?

    _____

    _____

9. Do you think the NCBC has affected other aspects of his/her life? If so, how and what areas?

    _____

    _____

NCBC Family/Staff Satisfaction Survey   Page 3

10. On a scale from 1 to 5, where 1 is not at all interested and 5 is always or very interested, rate the level of enthusiasm your family member or consumer shows towards the book club.

        1   2   3   4   5

Please give an example: _____

_____

11. Rating from 1 to 5, how do you think the member feels about meeting in the café or bookstore?

        1   2   3   4   5

12. On a scale from 1 to 5, where 1 is not at all satisfied and 5 is completely satisfied, how satisfied is your family member with his/her social life?

        1   2   3   4   5

13. Again, on a scale from 1 to 5, how satisfied is your family member with his/her degree of community participation?

        1   2   3   4   5

14. On a scale from 1 to 5, where 1 is not interested and 5 is always interested, how much interest does your family member show in reading *now*?

        1   2   3   4   5

15. On a scale from 1 to 5, where 1 is no enjoyment and 5 is much enjoyment, how much enjoyment does your family member derive from reading?

        1   2   3   4   5

16. What would you change about the book club?

_____

_____

17. Are there any other thoughts you would like to share about the NCBC?

_____

_____

THANK YOU very much for your time. Your responses are very helpful to us.

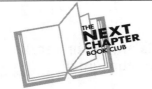

Next Chapter Book Club
Questions for Member Interviews

Name of NCBC Member: _____ Date of Interview: _____

1. How did you hear about the Next Chapter Book Club?

   _____

2. Why were you interested in joining the Next Chapter Book Club?

   _____

3. What do you enjoy most about the club?

   _____

4. Is there anything you would change about the club?

   _____

5. How has the book club helped you with your reading?

   _____

6. How often did you read before you joined the club?

   _____

7. What kinds of things do you like to read?

   _____

8. How old were you when you first learned to read?

   _____

NCBC Questions for Member Interviews   Page 2

9.   Tell me what it was like for you in school.

_____

_____

10. Tell me something about your work experience.

_____

_____

11. How does the book club relate to your job or other aspects of your life?

_____

_____

12. Can you tell me about the book we're reading? (*name of book*)

_____

_____

13. Do you have anything in common with the leading characters?

_____

_____

14. What would you tell someone who is thinking about joining a club?

_____

_____

15. Is there anything else you would like to share with us?

_____

_____

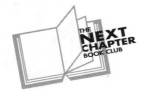

Next Chapter Book Club
Chuckie's Questionnaire

Name _____ Date _____

BIG YES	Little Yes	Little No	BIG NO

1. Do you like the book club?

   BIG YES   **Little Yes**   **Little No**   **BIG NO**

2. Do you like your facilitator?

   BIG YES   **Little Yes**   **Little No**   **BIG NO**

3. Do you like the book you're currently reading?

   BIG YES   **Little Yes**   **Little No**   **BIG NO**

4. Do you like where your book club meets every week?

   BIG YES   **Little Yes**   **Little No**   **BIG NO**

5. Are people in the bookstore friendly?

   BIG YES   **Little Yes**   **Little No**   **BIG NO**

6. Do you think your reading has improved since you joined the book club?

   BIG YES   **Little Yes**   **Little No**   **BIG NO**

7. Do you think you have more friends since you joined the book club?

   BIG YES   **Little Yes**   **Little No**   **BIG NO**

8. Do you think you are more comfortable in public places than before you started book club?

   BIG YES   **Little Yes**   **Little No**   **BIG NO**

NCBC Chuckie's Questionnaire   Page 2

9. Do you know anyone you could ask to join a book club? Who?

    _____

    _____

10. What would you suggest changing about your book club?

    _____

    _____

11. Is there anything I can do to help you?

    _____

    _____

12. Is there anything else you would like to tell me?

    _____

    _____

Thank you very much for your time. Your answers will really help us.

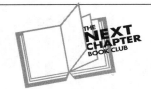

Next Chapter Book Club
Questions for Facilitator Interviews

Name of Facilitator: _____ Date of Interview: _____

1. How did you hear about the NCBC?

    _____

    _____

2. What interested you in becoming an NCBC facilitator?

    _____

    _____

3. How did your experience as a facilitator compare with what you expected?

    _____

    _____

4. How well did the training prepare you? Is there anything you would change about it?

    _____

    _____

5. Who in your club made the most progress reading? Please provide an example or two.

    _____

    _____

6. What strategy did you use that was most successful in helping members with reading?

    _____

    _____

7. How did participating in the NCBC change your ideas about literacy?

    _____

    _____

NCBC Questions for Facilitator Interviews   Page 2

8. Have you participated in book clubs yourself? If so tell us about that experience.

    _____

    _____

9. How would you describe the social interactions in your group? Please provide an example.

    _____

    _____

10. What did you do to promote social interactions between members?

    _____

    _____

11. What strategy was most successful to promote friendships among members?

    _____

    _____

12. How would you describe the host site staff or customers' reaction to your group?

    _____

    _____

13. How did this experience relate to your job or other aspects of your life?

    _____

    _____

14. What is the funniest thing that happened in your club?

    _____

    _____

15. What would you say to someone who is thinking about becoming an NCBC facilitator?

    _____

    _____

16. Is there anything else you would like to share with us?

    _____

    _____

Appendix O

Next Chapter Book Club
Community Inclusion Survey for Members BEFORE Book Club

Name of Member: _____ Date of Interview: _____

<u>Community Inclusion Survey questions</u> (from Neighbourhood Youth Inventory, Chipuer et al., 1999):

Circle your answer.

1. I live in a safe community.

    BIG YES   **Little Yes**   **Little No**   **BIG NO**   **Don't know**

2. People in my community pitch in to help each other.

    BIG YES   **Little Yes**   **Little No**   **BIG NO**   **Don't know**

3. I feel OK asking for help from my neighbors.

    BIG YES   **Little Yes**   **Little No**   **BIG NO**   **Don't know**

4. I have good support in my community.

    BIG YES   **Little Yes**   **Little No**   **BIG NO**   **Don't know**

5. I enjoy doing things with other people.

    BIG YES   **Little Yes**   **Little No**   **BIG NO**   **Don't know**

6. There is not much to do in my community.

    BIG YES   **Little Yes**   **Little No**   **BIG NO**   **Don't know**

7. I have friends I like to do things with.

    BIG YES   **Little Yes**   **Little No**   **BIG NO**   **Don't know**

8. I have friends to talk to on the telephone.

    BIG YES   **Little Yes**   **Little No**   **BIG NO**   **Don't know**

9. I feel comfortable going out to stores and restaurants.

    BIG YES   **Little Yes**   **Little No**   **BIG NO**   **Don't know**

NCBC Community Inclusion Survey for Members BEFORE Book Club   Page 2

10. Sometimes I feel lonely.

BIG YES   **Little Yes**   **Little No**   **BIG NO**   **Don't know**

11. I like going to do things outside my home.

BIG YES   **Little Yes**   **Little No**   **BIG NO**   **Don't know**

Open-ended questions:

12. How safe or scared do you feel when you are out doing things?

_____

_____

13. How happy do you feel when you are out doing things?

_____

_____

14. What makes you nervous when you are out doing things?

_____

_____

15. Who helps you most when you are out doing things?

_____

_____

16. What does that person do to help you?

_____

_____

17. Do you feel OK asking other people for help?

_____

_____

18. How nice are people to you when you are out doing things like shopping or going to the movies?

_____

_____

19. What other activities do you do outside your house? (such as clubs, sports, classes, church, etc.)

_____

_____

20. How would you feel about doing more things outside your house?

_____

_____

21. What kinds of things would you like to do?

_____

_____

22. What does it mean to you to have a good neighbor (someone who lives close to where you live)?

_____

_____

Appendix P

Next Chapter Book Club
Community Inclusion-Location Survey for Members AFTER Book Club

Name of Member: _____ Date of Interview: _____

<u>Community Inclusion Survey questions</u> (from Neighbourhood Youth Inventory, Chipuer et al., 1999):

Circle your answer.

1. I live in a safe community.

    BIG YES   **Little Yes**   **Little No**   **BIG NO**   **Don't know**

2. People in my community pitch in to help each other.

    BIG YES   **Little Yes**   **Little No**   **BIG NO**   **Don't know**

3. I feel OK asking for help from my neighbors.

    BIG YES   **Little Yes**   **Little No**   **BIG NO**   **Don't know**

4. I have good support in my community.

    BIG YES   **Little Yes**   **Little No**   **BIG NO**   **Don't know**

5. I enjoy doing things with other people.

    BIG YES   **Little Yes**   **Little No**   **BIG NO**   **Don't know**

6. There is not much to do in my community.

    BIG YES   **Little Yes**   **Little No**   **BIG NO**   **Don't know**

7. I have friends I like to do things with.

    BIG YES   **Little Yes**   **Little No**   **BIG NO**   **Don't know**

8. I have friends to talk to on the telephone.

    BIG YES   **Little Yes**   **Little No**   **BIG NO**   **Don't know**

9. I feel comfortable going out to stores and restaurants.

    BIG YES   **Little Yes**   **Little No**   **BIG NO**   **Don't know**

NCBC Community Inclusion-Location Survey for Members AFTER Book Club   Page 2

10. Sometimes I feel lonely.

  BIG YES   **Little Yes**   **Little No**   **BIG NO**   **Don't know**

11. I like going to do things outside my home.

  BIG YES   **Little Yes**   **Little No**   **BIG NO**   **Don't know**

<u>NCBC Location Survey questions</u>:

12. It is easy for me to get transportation to the book club meetings.

  BIG YES   **Little Yes**   **Little No**   **BIG NO**   **Don't know**

13. It is easy for me to get in and out of the store where my book club meets.

  BIG YES   **Little Yes**   **Little No**   **BIG NO**   **Don't know**

14. My book club meetings are held in a safe store.

  BIG YES   **Little Yes**   **Little No**   **BIG NO**   **Don't know**

15. I like the store where my book club meets.

  BIG YES   **Little Yes**   **Little No**   **BIG NO**   **Don't know**

16. The people who work where my book club meets make me feel good.

  BIG YES   **Little Yes**   **Little No**   **BIG NO**   **Don't know**

17. People at the book club store are friendly and nice to me.

  BIG YES   **Little Yes**   **Little No**   **BIG NO**   **Don't know**

18. People who sit at tables near my book club are friendly and nice to me.

  BIG YES   **Little Yes**   **Little No**   **BIG NO**   **Don't know**

19. I have made new friends in the book club.

  BIG YES   **Little Yes**   **Little No**   **BIG NO**   **Don't know**

20. I am comfortable ordering a drink or something to eat where my book club meets.

  BIG YES   **Little Yes**   **Little No**   **BIG NO**   **Don't know**

21. I sometimes feel uncomfortable at the store where my book club meets.

  BIG YES   **Little Yes**   **Little No**   **BIG NO**   **Don't know**

NCBC Community Inclusion-Location Survey for Members AFTER Book Club   Page 3

22. I feel comfortable getting up to go to the bathroom during book club meetings.

BIG YES   **Little Yes**   **Little No**   **BIG NO**   **Don't know**

<u>Open-ended questions</u>:

23. How does being at the book club make you feel?

_____

_____

24. What do you like about the store where your book club meets?

_____

_____

25. How safe or scared do you feel when you are out doing things?

_____

_____

26. How happy do you feel when you are out doing things?

_____

_____

27. What makes you nervous when you are out doing things?

_____

_____

28. Who helps you most when you are out doing things?

_____

_____

29. What does that person do to help you?

_____

_____

NCBC Community Inclusion-Location Survey for Members AFTER Book Club   Page 4

30. Do you feel OK asking other people for help?

_____

_____

31. How nice are people to you when you are out doing things like shopping or going to the movies?

_____

_____

32. What other activities do you do outside your house?
(such as clubs, sports, classes, church, etc.)

_____

_____

33. How would you feel about doing more things outside your house?

_____

_____

34. What kinds of things would you like to do?

_____

_____

35. What does it mean to you to have a good neighbor (someone who lives close to where you live)?

_____

_____

Next Chapter Book Club
Community Living Attitudes Scale (Adapted)

Short Form
David Henry, Christopher Keys, and David Jopp (1999)

Name: _____ Date of Interview: _____

> ***Directions:*** **Indicate the extent to which you agree with the following statements according to this scale:**
>
> **1 = Disagree strongly   4 = Agree somewhat**
> **2 = Disagree moderately   5 = Agree moderately**
> **3 = Disagree somewhat   6 = Agree strongly**

1. People with mental retardation should not be allowed to marry and have children.   1 2 3 4 5 6

2. A person would be foolish to marry a person with mental retardation.   1 2 3 4 5 6

3. People with mental retardation can plan meetings and conferences without assistance from others.   1 2 3 4 5 6

4. People with mental retardation can be trusted to handle money responsibly.   1 2 3 4 5 6

5. The opinion of a person with mental retardation should carry more weight than those of family members and professionals in decisions affecting that person.   1 2 3 4 5 6

6. Sheltered workshops for people with mental retardation are essential.   1 2 3 4 5 6

7. Increased spending on programs for people with mental retardation is a waste of tax dollars.   1 2 3 4 5 6

NCBC Community Living Attitudes Scale (Adapted)   Page 2

8. Homes and services for people with mental   1 2 3 4 5 6
    retardation downgrade the neighborhoods they
    are in.

9. People with mental retardation are a burden on   1 2 3 4 5 6
    society.

10. Homes and services for people with mental   1 2 3 4 5 6
    retardation should be kept out of residential
    neighborhoods.

11. People with mental retardation need someone to   1 2 3 4 5 6
    plan their activities for them.

12. People with mental retardation do not need to   1 2 3 4 5 6
    make choices about the things they will do each
    day.

13. People with mental retardation can be productive   1 2 3 4 5 6
    members of society.

14. People with mental retardation have goals for   1 2 3 4 5 6
    their lives like other people.

15. People with mental retardation can have close   1 2 3 4 5 6
    personal relationships just like everyone else.

16. People with mental retardation should live in   1 2 3 4 5 6
    sheltered facilities because of the dangers of life
    in the community.

17. People with mental retardation usually should be   1 2 3 4 5 6
    in group homes or other facilities where they can
    have the help and support of staff.

---

1 = Disagree strongly	4 = Agree somewhat
2 = Disagree moderately	5 = Agree moderately
3 = Disagree somewhat	6 = Agree strongly

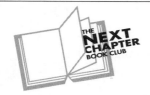

Appendix R

Lyons, IL

Unique book club started for young adults

By Wendy Foster
Western Springs Suburban Life
Wed Aug 08, 2007, 01:32 PM CDT

Western Springs, IL –

There's a new book club in town. Each Monday this summer, a group of four young adults have been meeting at the Borders in La Grange to discuss Robert Louis Stevenson's "Treasure Island." This group is a bit unique in that each member uses an augmentative or alternative communication device. The group was started by Western Springs residents Pam Harris and her teenage son, Josh. Josh has Rubinstein-Taybi syndrome, a genetic disorder that is characterized by impairments in cognitive processing. Because functional speech is difficult for Josh, he relies on assistive technology in order to communicate. He and his mother work to increase awareness about the use of augmentative and assistive devices used to help individuals with disabilities to communicate. His mother and Dr. Jill Senner founded Augmentative Communication Technical Supports in order to operate programs and opportunities such as the book club.

Harris said that the club is modeled after Next Chapter Book Club which was founded at Ohio State University. This program is designed to give adolescents and adults with intellectual disabilities the opportunity to read and discuss books, while socializing with their friends. Harris said that she learned about the program through a local Ups for Downs chapter, a nonprofit organization comprised predominantly of parents of individuals with Down syndrome. Ups for Downs is funding training for Next Chapter Book Club for area organizations that provide services to individuals with disabilities.

Harris said that operating the book club has required significant preparation and special tools. The text for "Treasure Island," she said, has been "carefully written and edited to meet the needs of those struggling, or the early reader. Those barriers including language, syntax, vocabulary and dialogue which would make the book difficult have been removed. This has really contributed to the success of the program," Harris said. A company that provides adaptive learning materials compiled a kit including a hard copy of "Treasure Island," a CD of the book to listen to, and a computer disk of the book which highlights the words as they're being read.

Harris said that the reading group tackles one chapter each week. "They all read the chapter before we meet," she said.

Then each individual is responsible for sharing a page in whatever method he/she communicates. For instance, she said Josh uses a device which actually generates speech from words he's typed in.

"This means that he's entered the page word by word into his device," she said.

Another member, she said, reads aloud on his laptop computer and everyone follows along.

"He moves the cursor along as the computer reads his part aloud. Everyone is reading a page at a time, at their level of comfort. It's not a test. It's recreational, social reading," Harris said.

After taking turns reading, the book club members are asked four to five content questions.

"And Dr. Senner always has one question that the book club member can relate to a personal experience," Harris said.

Harris said that there are three basic objectives of the book club: to improve literacy skills and social connections, to increase the inclusion of individuals with communication devices in community settings, and to improve lifelong learning opportunities. She feels that thus far the book club has been a success. "The group has taken on its own personality. It's so exciting," she said.

Harris said that the book club meetings will continue until the book has been completed. "Everyone signed a contract that they'd stick with it for the whole book and there are 10 chapters," she said.

For further information visit www.actsIL.org.

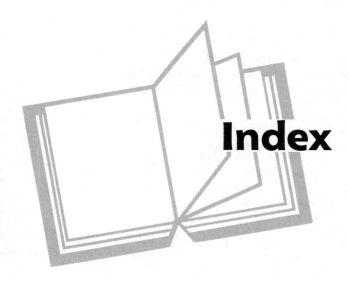

Index

Page numbers in italics indicate tables and figures

Adult-based learning, 8
Affiliates, Next Chapter Book Club (NCBC), *15*, 15–20
Affiliate training workshops, 21–26
    book selection and, 24–25
    demonstrations and, 26
    facilitators and, 24
    feedback and, 26
    fees for, 25
    host sites and, 24
    location of training for, 23
    preparations for, 22–25
    sample schedule, *25*
Background, Next Chapter Book Club (NCBC), ix, 1, 49–51
Baldini, Deborah, viii
Banks, Aliscia, 86
Beneficiaries, 6
Book selections, 24–25, 76, 163
Cataldi, Susan, 17
Certificate of Accomplishment, member 172
Chuckie's Questionnaire, 182
Club agreements, 52–53
Club composition, 137–38
Club operations, 135–37
Community activities, *12*
Community inclusion
    literacy and, 7, 8
    Literacy Survey for Members After Book Club, 189
    Literacy Survey for Members Before Book Club, 186
    members and, x
    model, Next Chapter Book Club (NCBC), 10–13
    strategies, 73–74, 114–20
    surveys, 130–31
Community Living Attitudes Scale (Adapted), 193
Community settings, 13
Conventionally literate, 2

Cooley, Steve, 82
ECO-NCBC Literacy Observations, 128, 174
Emergent literacy skills, 3, 104
Emergent readers, learning process for, 95
Facilitator interviews, questions for, 129–30, 184
Facilitators, 55–66
    benefits of volunteering and, 56–57
    co-facilitators and, 58–59
    non-student, 61
    participation, 2
    position description, 167
    profiles of, 62–66
    prospective, 62
    recruiting volunteers and, 55, 184
    student, 60–61
    volunteers and, 5, 57–60
Facilitators, duties of, 67–78
    attendance/group membership and, 75
    balanced/reciprocal communications and, 71
    behavioral issues and, 74–75
    book selection and, 76, 163
    community inclusion and, 73–74
    conduct self-evaluation and, 68–69
    end-of-book surveys and, 76
    Facilitator Intake Form and, 68, 166
    group process guidelines and, 74
    group tasks and, 77
    guidelines and, 69
    introductions and, 69
    literacy/communication strategies and, 70–72, 95-120
    managing book club and, 75–76
    monthly reports and, 76, 168
    motivation and, 67–68
    phone reminders and, 75
    preparations and, 68–69

primary roles and, 70, 167
program coordinator and, 67, 76
recruiting and, 77–78
social connections and, 72–73
supporting members and, 70
verbal/nonverbal communications and, 71
working with co-facilitator and, 77
Families Helping Families of Greater New Orleans, Inc., 18, 86
Families/support staff, roles of, 91–94
Families/support staff/service coordinators, 121–22
Family members/support staff evaluations, 128–29
Family/Staff Expectation Survey, 128–29, 175
Family/Staff Satisfaction Survey, 128–29, 177
Ferguson, Philip, vii
Fish, Tom, x–xi, 1, 5, 18, 85, 133
Five-Level Scale of Literacy Skills, 38–43, 127–28, 173
Funding sources/community organizations, 124–25
Graff, Vicki, xiii, 5
Grosh, Vicki, 85
Group dynamics, 138–39
Host sites, 79–89
    affiliates and, 5
    affiliate training workshops and, 24
    approaching manager of, 87–88
    benefits to, 79–80, 80
    disadvantages of, 82–83
    exceptions rule and, 84–85
    finding, 34
    function of, 79
    members and, 11
    model, Next Chapter Book Club (NCBC) and, 11, 12
    private homes and, 82
    profiles of, 85–87
    profiles of a manager, 88–89
    program coordinator and, 30–31, 81
    responding to Next Chapter Book Clubs, 80–81
    restaurants and, 83–84
    selecting, 87
    strategies and, 115
Independent literacy skills, 9, 173
Individual Service Plan (ISP), 93
Input/feedback, 91
Intellectual disabilities (ID), vii, ix, xv, 1, 7, 10, 11, 124
Leaders, 5–6
Library of Next Chapter Book Club books, 163
Literacy, 8–9
Literacy evaluations, 127–28, 173
Literacy Observations, ECO-NCBC, 174
Literacy skills, 95
Marketing/promoting, 121–25
Marketing tools, 92
McMullen, Nann, 86, 87
Member End-of-Book Survey, 171
Member Intake Form, 165
Member interviews, questions for, 129, 180, 182
Members, Next Chapter Book Club (NCBC), 37–47
    Certificate of Accomplishment, 172
    expectations of, 56
    Five-Level Scale of Literacy Skills and, 38–43
    peer activity leaders (PALs), 43–47
    profiles of, 38–43

questionnaires of, 53–54, 180, 182
recruiting of, 38
responsibilities of, 51–52
rights of, 51
surveys of inclusion, 186, 189
Model, Next Chapter Book Club (NCBC), 7, 7–13
    community inclusion and, 8, 10–13, 186, 189
    host sites and, 11, 12
    literacy and, 8–9
    reciprocal relationship, 13
    social connections and, 10
National Institute for Literacy, 8
National Reading Panel (NRP), 95
Neal, Sue, 18–19
Next Chapter Book Club (NCBC)
    club agreements and, 52–53
    objectives, ix-x, 2, 8
    Paula Rabidoux on, xi–xii
    Tom Fish on, x–xi
Ober, Jillian, 5
The Ohio State University Nisonger Center, vii, x, 1, 5, 63, 146
Opportunity Enterprises, Inc., 16
Organization, 5
Organizational chart, 4
Palmer, Chris, 85
Participants, 2
Participation, 133
Peer activity leaders (PALs), 43–47
Post, Stephen, 56
Premise, 1
Program coordinators, 27–35
    description of, 27
    facilitators and, 29, 67, 76
    host sites and, 30–31, 81
    Member Intake Forms and, 29, 165
    Monthly Facilitator Report and, 30, 168
    recruiting and, 28–29
    retaining facilitators and, 30
    scheduling and, 30–31
    training and, 29–30
Program evaluations, 127–31
Questions for Facilitator Interviews form, 184
Questions for Member Interviews form, 180
Rabidoux, Paula, xi–xii, 5, 11
Reading levels, description of, 3
Self-advocacy, x
Self-determination, ix
Service agencies/advocacy organizations, 123
Snook, Jack, 17–18
Social activities, 10. See also Strategies/activities
Social context, 8
Social interactions, 58, 59, 106–14
Spontaneous activities, 12
Strategies/activities, 95–120
    address books and, 118
    autobiographies and, 110–11
    building sentences and, 100
    celebrations and, 110
    choosing books and, 113
    community inclusion and, 114–20
    crossword puzzles and, 101

echo reading and, 104
encouraging reading and, 95–106
facilitator reading and, 96
field trips and, 116
games and, 102–03
home/apartment drawings and, 118–19
host sites and, 115
identifying community locations and, 119
increasing comprehension and, 96–98
increasing participation/fluency and, 104–06
increasing phonemic awareness and, 102–03
increasing vocabulary and, 98–102
libraries and, 115–16
newspapers and, 117–18
past week experiences and, 117
personal stories and, 97
phonemic awareness and, 102-03, 107
phone tree and, 109
poetry and, 98
punctuation and, 98
round table and, 97–98
sharing and, 113
social interactions and, 10, 106–14
special considerations and, 139–41
specific questions and, 96–97
spell/write words and, 99
support and, 5–6
theme week and, 112
use of memories/current events and, 110
using dictionaries and, 100
word lists and, 99
Support strategies, 5–6
Tarquinio, Jean, 16–17
Tebbe, Eddie, 18
Transportation, source of, 91
United Cerebral Palsy (Pittsburgh, PA), 17
Vocational Rehabilitation, 8
Volunteers. *See* Facilitators
Western Springs Suburban Life article, 195

About the Authors

Tom Fish, PhD, LISW, Program Director

Dr. Tom Fish has his Masters degree in Social Work from Boston University and PhD in Rehabilitation Counseling from The Ohio State University. He directs the Family Support and Employment program at The Ohio State University Nisonger Center for Excellence in Developmental Disabilities. Dr. Fish is involved with teaching, interdisciplinary training, and program development activities. His research and clinical involvement centers around sibling support, self-advocacy, community integration, and school-to-work transition. Dr. Fish serves on the board of the Central Ohio Down Syndrome Association and was a recipient of a Mary E. Switzer Research Fellowship from the National Institute on Disability and Rehabilitation Research.

Paula Rabidoux, PhD/CCC, Literacy Specialist

For the past twenty years, Dr. Paula Rabidoux's research and clinical interests have focused on the issues involved in literacy learning for children and adults with communicative and cognitive impairments. She recently developed a model of Interactive-to-Independent Literacy that includes all levels of literacy participants. (Kaderavek and Rabidoux, 2004). This model has served as the theoretical foundation for the design and implementation of treatment programs for children and adults with a variety of communication impairments; it has also provided the literacy strategies for the Next Chapter Book Clubs. Dr. Rabidoux is also the training coordinator for the LEND program at Nisonger Center at The Ohio State University.

Jillian Ober, MA, CRC, Program Manager

Ms. Jillian Ober received her Masters degree in Rehabilitation Counseling from The Ohio State University in June 2004. At the Nisonger Center, Ms. Ober manages programs that emphasize community inclusion and lifelong learning for adolescents and adults with intellectual and developmental disabilities. These programs include Young Adult Transition Corps, an AmeriCorps program promoting successful transitions from school to adult life for young adults with disabilities, as well as the Ohio AmeriCorps Inclusion Project. Ms. Ober conducts training workshops and coordinates technical support for the NCBC's affiliates outside Columbus, Ohio. She now also coordinates all the clubs operating in the Columbus area.

Vicki Graff, BA, BEd, Program Manager

Ms. Vicki Graff earned a Bachelor of Arts in geography and social sciences and a Bachelor of Education in geography and elementary education, both from the University of Toronto, Canada. Ms. Graff has more than 30 years of experience in publishing, marketing, communications, advertising, public relations, administration, teaching, and training in a variety of academic, non-profit, and corporate settings. Her special interests are in health science, nutrition, and education. Ms. Graff came to The OSU Nisonger Center in 2005 to promote and publicize the Next Chapter Book Club. She coordinated all the clubs operating in the Columbus area from August 2007 through June 2009. She now manages marketing and communications for the Nisonger Center.